WHAT
A YEAR
IT WAS!

1962

A walk back in time to revisit
what life was like in the year that
has special meaning for you...

*Congratulations
and
Best Wishes*

To

From

DEDICATION

To My Business Partner and Dear Friend, Jack Nadel

You are indeed a rare and remarkable man and I'm privileged to have been able to work so closely with you all these years. Thank you so much for all you've done and continue to do.

With Love and Deep Appreciation,
Bev

Series Created By • Beverly Cohn

Designers • Peter Hess & Marguerite Jones

Research • Laurie Cohn

Special thanks to Kenny Bookbinder for his invaluable help with the Sports section.

CONTENTS

POLITICS AND WORLD EVENTS 5

PEOPLE 25

HUMAN INTEREST 47

ENTERTAINMENT 65

FASHION 115

NEW PRODUCTS AND INVENTIONS 125

SCIENCE 131

MEDICINE 139

BUSINESS 149

DISASTERS 157

SPORTS 159

POLITICS 1962

& WORLD EVENTS

KENNEDY DECLARES ARMS BLOCKADE AGAINST CUBA

In the most critical period in history since the end of World War II, world peace is threatened as Red puppet **Fidel Castro** and the Russians turn Cuba into an island fortress.

U.S. planes spot missile installations aimed at key points in the Western Hemisphere and bring back evidence of a weapons build-up that moves the Organization of American States and the Western Allies to back **President Kennedy** unanimously when he declares an arms blockade of Cuba and issues an ultimatum.

WHAT A YEAR IT WAS!

continued

1962

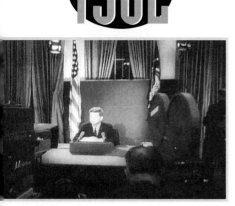

" To halt this defensive build-up, a strict quarantine on all offensive military equipment under shipment to Cuba is being initiated. "

" All ships of any kind bound to Cuba, from whatever nation or port, will, if found to contain cargoes of offensive weapons, be turned back. "

In the face of U.S. determination, the Soviets dismantle their missiles and bombers and ship them home. It is a capitulation for Moscow. Democratic nations have served notice on the Russians that any aggressive threat in the Western Hemisphere will not be tolerated.

WHAT A YEAR IT WAS!

ON THE BRINK

CUBAN CRISIS TIMELINE

1962

AUGUST

President Kennedy confirms reports that several thousand Soviet technicians and large quantities of supplies are pouring into Cuba.

SEPTEMBER

Soviets announce they will arm and train Cuban military personnel.

Senate resolution serving notice that the U.S. will use military force if necessary against a Cuban threat to U.S. security is approved by the U.S. House.

Cuba is the primary concern of the Kennedy Administration and Congress grants the President power to call up 150,000 military reservists.

In an address to the nation, President Kennedy announces a naval and air "quarantine" on shipment of offensive military supplies to Cuba.

Castro mobilizes as the U.S. orders interception of 25 Soviet vessels in defiance of Moscow threat.

OCTOBER

Soviet Premier Khrushchev orders ships to avoid blockade and suggests summit to avoid nuclear war.

Moscow offers to dismantle bases in Cuba if the U.S. disbands bases in Turkey.

In a raiding vessel manned by exiles, a Cuban patrol boat is sunk off the coast of Cuba.

The Soviet Union challenges the right of the U.S. to stop shipments of arms to Cuba and says the Kennedy Administration is risking nuclear war.

The Council of the Organization of American States votes unanimously to authorize the use of armed force to prevent shipments of offensive weapons to Cuba.

The British foreign office accuses the Soviet Union of duplicity and supports the U.S. blockade.

Acting U.N. Secretary-General U Thant asks the United States to cease the Cuban blockade and asks Russia to stop sending missiles.

The U.S. stands its ground that the blockade will continue as long as there is a missile threat.

The U.S. Navy boards a Soviet-chartered freighter en route to Havana and after inspection allows it to proceed.

Khrushchev sends a letter to President Kennedy offering to remove military bases in Cuba under U.N. supervision and the broadcast of a second letter demands that the U.S. take corresponding action in Turkey.

A U-2 reconnaissance plane is missing and presumed lost over Cuba.

Khrushchev agrees to dismantle Soviet installations in Cuba and arrange for a U.N. inspection team and in return he wants the U.S. to lift the blockade and join with other OAS nations in a commitment against invasion of Cuba.

U Thant flies to Cuba to confer with Prime Minister Castro on the details for a U.N. inspection of the dismantling of the Soviet missiles. The U.S. suspends its naval blockade and air surveillance during Thant's visit.

Castro tells U Thant that Cuba will not accept inspection of military installations unless the U.S. agrees to five conditions, one being evacuation of the U.S. naval base at Guantanamo Bay.

NOVEMBER

In a broadcast, Castro rejects any form of international inspection in Cuba.

President Kennedy announces that aerial photographs indicate Soviet missiles in Cuba are being crated and bases dismantled. U.S. surveillance will continue until a satisfactory means of inspection has been arranged.

Khrushchev announces that the U.S.S.R. has removed all its rockets from Cuba.

U.S. Navy ships intercept, but do not board, Soviet cargo vessels north of Havana and photographed objects believed to be missiles are on the way back to the U.S.S.R.

Chinese Communist Party criticizes Khrushchev for Cuban compromise indicating a widening breach between China and the U.S.S.R.

President Kennedy announces the lifting of the naval blockade of Cuba following assurances from Khrushchev that all of its jet bombers in Cuba will be removed within 30 days.

U.S. Air Force releases over 14,000 men who were called to active duty in October because of the Cuban missile crisis.

DECEMBER

In keeping with Khrushchev's agreement, 42 Soviet jet bombers are being shipped out of Cuba and returned to the U.S.S.R.

President Kennedy, accompanied by his wife, fly to Florida to review the Cuban invasion brigade captured in the Bay of Pigs attack and tells them that *"Cuba shall one day be free again."*

1962

GERMANS FLEE DESPITE WALL

The wall of shame in Berlin is one year old.

Last year East German Communists built the wall to try to stop the number of people fleeing to freedom in West Berlin.

The Reds are constantly at work reinforcing and guarding the wall, but people still find a way to escape to the West.

Some people make it and some don't. The civilized world cries "shame" when East German guards shoot a teenager, Peter Fechter, and then leave him to die.

They remove his body, but they will never remove him as a symbol to the angered Germans.

Demonstrators, held back by guards, vent their wrath on buses carrying Russian guards to a Soviet war memorial and stone the honor guards at the memorial. The Soviets lodge a formal protest.

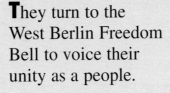

They turn to the West Berlin Freedom Bell to voice their unity as a people.

The Allies continue to stand firm in Berlin and the Germans make a national hero of **U.S. General Lucius Clay** who continues to be a leading spokesman for German freedom.

1962

NO MORE WAR FOR FRANCE,
Peace At Last

France is at peace for the first time since 1939.

After seven years of bitter fighting between French and Algerian rebel forces, the war in Algeria comes to an end as 98% of French voters endorse the Algerian cease-fire in a referendum authorizing French President Charles de Gaulle to enforce the settlement.

Despite terrorist acts by the French Secret Army Organization, Algeria wins its freedom ending 132 years of outside rule.

Ahmed Ben Bella, organizer of the insurrection that led to independence, is elected premier of Algeria and soon finds himself beset with a score of problems.

As the new nation faces economic collapse, Ben Bella turns to President de Gaulle for help. Back in France, de Gaulle calls for a national referendum on a constitutional amendment which would change the method of electing the president from the electoral college to direct popular vote.

In Paris, General RAOUL SALAN, former leader of the French Algerian Secret Army Organization, is sentenced to life in prison.

◦∫∫◦

30 people arrested in Paris in a plot to kill DE GAULLE.

◦∫∫◦

Hundreds of Europeans flee the violence in Algiers.

◦∫∫◦

Algeria joins the United Nations.

The Irish Republican Army announces the end of its campaign of violence against the partition of Ireland.

Great Britain releases political prisoners following IRA peace offer.

Dutch sign pact granting Indonesia rule over New Guinea.

French President de Gaulle names Georges Pompidou to succeed Michel Debre as premier.

For the first time in modern French history, one group has a clear majority as supporters of President de Gaulle win control of France's national assembly.

Monaco's unwillingness to alter its status as a tax haven results in France abrogating its 1951 convention with Monaco.

Canada collects a $1 billion loan from the United States and the United Kingdom to help halt its economic slide.

1962 — The Arms Race

In a nationwide address, JFK warns that he will resume U.S. nuclear atmospheric tests unless the Soviets agree to an iron-clad treaty barring all tests.

Soviet Premier Nikita S. Khrushchev's call for an 18-nation meeting to discuss disarmament is rejected by the United States and Great Britain.

Khrushchev

JFK orders resumption of atmospheric atom testing. The U.S. declares it is ready to use nuclear arms in Germany to protect its vital interests in Berlin.

- The U.N.-sponsored disarmament conference opens in Geneva, Switzerland with 17 nations participating.

- The U.S. submits a three-stage program on disarmament.

- In Geneva, Russia, the U.S. and the United Kingdom suspend arms talks indefinitely which have been ongoing for over three years.

- U.S. once again turns down Soviet bid for new Geneva arms talks.

U Thant
is unanimously elected U.N. Secretary-General by the General Assembly.

MOSCOW ACCUSES ISRAELI

diplomats of using synagogues for espionage activities.

THE FIRST SECRETARY

of the U.S. Embassy in Moscow is expelled on spying charges, the second U.S. diplomat ordered out of the Soviet Union within seven days.

FOLLOWING THE REMOVAL of

a U.S. tank near the East-West Berlin wall, the Soviets withdraw 12 tanks.

GREAT BRITAIN, FRANCE AND

THE U.S. lodge protests to the Soviets against the dangerous Soviet harassment of their flights into West Berlin.

THE SOVIET GOVERNMENT

lowers military draft age from 18 to 17.

MOSCOW SAYS it will defend

China against any invasion.

U-2 PILOT GARY FRANCIS POWERS

freed by Russia in exchange for U.S.-held Soviet spy Rudolph I. Abel, sentenced in the U.S. in 1957.

U-2 pilot Powers on trial in the Soviet Union, 1960.

1962

OSWALD MOSLEY CAUSES RIOTS IN ENGLAND

Sir Oswald Mosley (left) tries to bring his union movement message to Manchester, England where a melee quickly breaks out as followers of the avowed fascist run into some locals who believe in democracy over totalitarianism.

The "Mosleyites" move into London to hold their rally in Dalston, scene of many Mosley riots in pre-war days. Things are not much quieter on Ridley Row than they were in Manchester.

Undaunted, Sir Oswald walks to a truck to begin his talk and the sky falls in. The bobbies have their hands full rescuing the man who tried to make the black shirts popular in England.

14

WHAT A YEAR IT WAS!

Sir Oswald continues to his platform as the police hold back jeering crowds.

Despite being a fast master at invective and rebel rousing, he can't make himself heard above the din and finally gives up.

As Mosley leaves the platform under heavy police guard fighting breaks out again. Patience exhausted, police begin to round up the ringleaders and 54 people are arrested. Several are injured but Mosley comes through unscathed.

After more than 300 years as a British possession, agreement is signed to grant independence to **JAMAICA**, making it an independent member of the British Commonwealth.

WHAT A YEAR IT WAS!

1962

Massachusetts Democrat **John W. McCormack** is elected Speaker of the House at the second session of the 87th Congress of the U.S.

Young Americans for Freedom choose Republican Senator **Barry Goldwater** as their presidential candidate in the 1964 elections.

In largest voter turnout for a non-election year, Democrats gain and **Edward Kennedy** wins Massachusetts Senate seat.

Richard Nixon launches his bid for governor of California by accusing Governor **Edmund G. Brown** of ignoring the threat of Communism.

Defeated California gubernatorial candidate **Richard Nixon** concedes, announcing *"You won't have Nixon to kick around anymore."*

A U.S. constitutional amendment to bar the poll tax as a requirement for voting in federal elections receives congressional approval.

Failing to register as an agent of the U.S.S.R. is a criminal act and costs the U.S. Communist Party $10,000 on each of the 12 counts.

U.S. State Department issues new regulations denying passports to members of the Communist Party.

President Kennedy *requests authority from Congress to spend up to $2 billion on expanded public works programs if unemployment figures indicate a recession.*

President Kennedy *asks U.S. Congress to authorize the tripling of the Peace Corps.*

In a special message to U.S. Congress, **President Kennedy** *asks for $1 billion to expand federal recreational areas.*

President Kennedy *calls for a consumer protection plan covering food, drugs, cosmetics and television sets.*

President Kennedy *signs a bill permitting stricter federal control over employee pension and welfare plans.*

President Kennedy *signs a bill authorizing the Peace Corps to expand to approximately 10,000 volunteers.*

President Kennedy *signs the Food and Agriculture Act of 1962 providing for some increased crop controls.*

President Kennedy *signs a bill authorizing a loan of $100 million to the United Nations to meet a financial crisis.*

Calling it unnecessary and undesirable, **President Kennedy** *rejects immediate federal income tax cuts.*

WHAT A YEAR IT WAS!

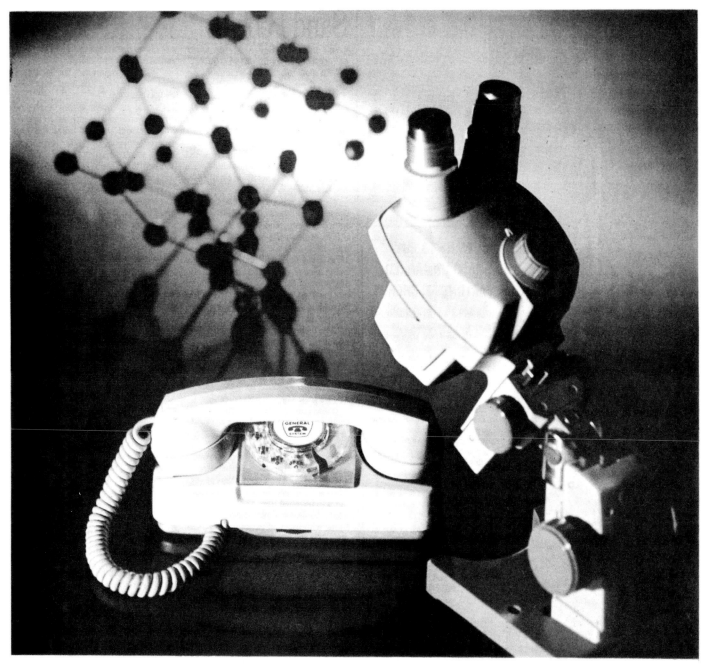

Eyeing the future through research

At Gen Tel, research works continuously to expand our horizons.  For instance, with room in the radio spectrum rapidly running out, scientists at General Telephone & Electronics Laboratories are helping to harness a new kind of light for tomorrow's communications. This "coherent" light is produced by a device called a gas laser. Now in the development stage, it may someday provide an almost limitless number of communications highways to meet tomorrow's ever-increasing needs. Progressive research such as this benefits everyone.

GENERAL TELEPHONE & ELECTRONICS

GENERAL SYSTEM / 730 Third Avenue, New York 17

GT&E SUBSIDIARIES: General Telephone Operating Companies in 32 states · General Telephone & Electronics Laboratories · General Telephone & Electronics International · General Telephone Directory Co. · Automatic Electric · Leich Electric · Lenkurt Electric · Electronic Secretary Industries · Sylvania Electric Products

17

KENNEDY SPEAKS REGARDING PRAYER IN SCHOOL

The first question at President Kennedy's news conference deals with a Supreme Court decision that a New York school prayer violates constitutional separation of church and state.

The President's statement is in the nature of an effort to calm the storm over the decision:

"Well, I haven't seen the measures in the Congress and you'd have to make a determination what the language was and what the effect it would have on the first amendment. The Supreme Court has made its judgment. A good many people obviously will disagree with it. Others will agree with it. But I think that it is important for us, if we are going to maintain our constitutional principle, that we support the Supreme Court decisions, even when we may not agree with them. In addition, we have, in this case, a very easy remedy and that is to pray ourselves. And I would think that it would be a welcome reminder to every American family that we can pray a good deal more at home, we can attend our churches with a good deal more fidelity and we can make the true meaning of prayer much more important in the lives of all of our children. That power is very much open to us. And I would hope that as a result of this decision, that all American parents will intensify their efforts at home."

1962

★ Vietnam & Indochina

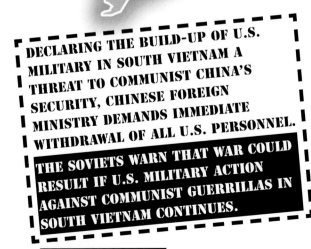

China

Vietnam

Laos

Cambodia

In an effort to destroy Viet Cong food supplies and to defoliate their hiding places in the jungle, "Operation Ranch Hand" begins which calls for the spraying of pesticides along a 70-mile route leading to Saigon.

Two Americans killed in Vietnam ambush north of Saigon.

U.S. Defense Secretary Robert McNamara reveals that U.S. military training personnel in South Vietnam have returned the fire of Communist guerrilla forces.

Nam Tha, royal government stronghold, captured by Pathet Lao rebels in Laos.

Ships and over 1,000 Marines are dispatched to Laos by President Kennedy to counter Communist gains.

4,000 U.S. troops are sent to Thailand to aid Laos.

Public gatherings without police authorization are banned in South Vietnam.

Calling it a clear breach of the cease-fire in Laos, President Kennedy condemns attacks by pro-Communist troops.

Headed by Prince Suvanna Phuma, a new coalition Laotian government is installed.

The last U.S. Marines are withdrawn from Thailand.

DECLARING THE BUILD-UP OF U.S. MILITARY IN SOUTH VIETNAM A THREAT TO COMMUNIST CHINA'S SECURITY, CHINESE FOREIGN MINISTRY DEMANDS IMMEDIATE WITHDRAWAL OF ALL U.S. PERSONNEL.

THE SOVIETS WARN THAT WAR COULD RESULT IF U.S. MILITARY ACTION AGAINST COMMUNIST GUERRILLAS IN SOUTH VIETNAM CONTINUES.

1962 India Wants To Be Neutral

India finds the path of neutralism a hard one in a world torn by strife. Red China pours troops over her northern frontier and India's people mobilize to meet the threat.

India has been ill prepared to defend herself and defense minister Krishna Menon is deposed.

The people donate their jewelry and life savings to the defense effort as their government seeks aid.

The West responds quickly to Prime Minister Nehru's appeal, but Russia's promises never materialize.

Neutralism seems to be withering.

By a vote of 56 to 42, the U.N. General Assembly votes against admission of Communist China.

MARX

MAO

A formal agreement is reached between the United States and Japan on the final settlement of U.S. post-war economic assistance to Japan.

10,000 refugees are to be returned to Communist China by the Hong Kong government.

Hong Kong puts up barbed wire fences to keep out illegal Chinese immigrants.

Taiwan offers to take in refugees from China.

President Kennedy says action will be taken to help Chinese refugees in Hong Kong immigrate to the U.S.

Mongolia

Korea

Japan

China

Tibet

Nepal

India

Burma

Laos

Thailand

Vietnam

Cambodia

Philippines

Ceylon

* Chinese and Indian troops clash on border.

* U.S. pledges to rush arms to India.

* In heavy border fighting, the Chinese push back the Indians.

* India is beaten in its war with Communist China which orders a cease-fire after militarily establishing a new border between India and Tibet.

1962

U.S.-owned phone system seized in BRAZIL.

ARGENTINA becomes the 14th Latin American country to break diplomatic ties with Cuba.

- Argentine President Arturo Frondizi to form a coalition with the military barring Peronists.
- Jose Maria Guido is sworn in as president after Argentine President Arturo Frondizi is deposed and arrested by the armed forces.
- The Argentine congress and all political parties are dissolved by President Guido.

CUBA begins trials of Bay of Pigs invaders.

- Cuba sentences over 1,000 invaders to 30 years in prison and asks for $62 million in ransom to buy their freedom.
- With Castro's asking price of $2,500,000 for the sick and wounded, 60 Cuban prisoners arrive in Miami.
- President Kennedy orders a ban on all U.S. trade with Cuba depriving Fidel Castro of $35 million in annual income.
- At the request of the United States, Cuba is banned from participating in the affairs of the Organization of American States but is permitted to remain a member.
- A $700 million trade agreement is signed between Cuba and the U.S.S.R.
- Cuban government nationalizes all privately-owned stores selling clothing, shoes and hardware except those run solely by the owners or their relatives.
- Cuban exiles shell a Havana suburb in a sea raid.
- In exchange for more than $50 million in food and medical supplies, Cuba begins releasing prisoners captured in the April 1961 Bay of Pigs invasion.

Israel to be supplied with short-range missiles by the U.S.

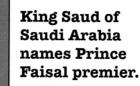

President Kennedy confers with King Saud on building a U.S. air base in Saudi Arabia.

King Saud of Saudi Arabia names Prince Faisal premier.

22

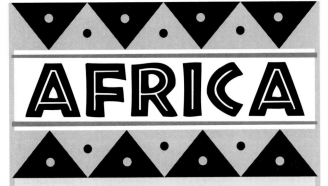

AFRICA

African common market is established.

•

The Republic of Rwanda and Kingdom of Burundi are formed, winning their independence from Belgium.

•

Uganda becomes the 110th member of the U.N.

•

The U.N. General Assembly votes to ask United Nations members to impose economic sanctions on South Africa until it abandons racial segregation.

•

19 Belgian Roman Catholic missionaries slain by marauding Congolese troops in northern Katanga.

•

U.N. forces are dispatched to the Congo to restore order in Stanleyville.

KATANGESE PRESIDENT MOISE TSHOMBE FLEES AS U.N. FORCES INVADE KATANGA AND CAPTURE THE CAPITAL CITY OF ELISABETHVILLE.

If you drive this car, you're going to have to get used to sharing its beauty with a lot of spectators. You really can't blame people for clustering around this new Grand Prix, can you? And it shouldn't bother you much, anyhow. You'll be too busy enjoying its utterly civilized road manners. A wider Wide-Track does it, along with a calm, collected ride. The vigorous Trophy V-8 humming away under the hood helps, too. But instead of just sitting there reading a list of GP joys, why don't you sample the whole package firsthand? Your Pontiac dealer's the man with the keys. He'll let the GP do its own selling—but we warn you: it's the most effective sales talk you ever heard. Make plans to listen in soon.

PONTIAC MOTOR DIVISION · GENERAL MOTORS CORPORATION

GP

PONTIAC GRAND PRIX

First Lady

Eleanor Roosevelt dies

Pictured here with her late husband, **President Franklin Delano Roosevelt**, death comes to **Eleanor Roosevelt**, one of the world's most extraordinary and beloved women.

Mrs. Roosevelt made the role of First Lady a dynamic one, as she walked with the great and the humble.

She spent her later years as an avid worker for peace through the United Nations and was adored by children visiting the family estate.

An international humanitarian, she leaves a legacy of accomplishment.

WHAT A YEAR IT WAS!

1962

Marilyn Monroe
Dies At Age 36

One of the most famous stars in Hollywood history is found dead in bed under circumstances that are in tragic contrast to her glamorous career as a comic talent, for on the surface she seemed to have such a zest for life.

Her international appeal took her all over the world, including a command appearance before Queen Elizabeth. Victor Mature stands at her right.

Marilyn entertained American GI's in Korea who made her their special pin-up girl.

WHAT A YEAR IT WAS!

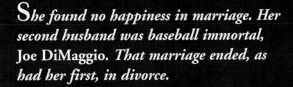

She found no happiness in marriage. Her second husband was baseball immortal, Joe DiMaggio. *That marriage ended, as had her first, in divorce.*

Her third husband was playwright Arthur Miller *and they too separated.*

Ms. Monroe played in 23 films since her debut in 1950, films that grossed over $200 million. The "Golden Girl" received 5,000 fan letters a week. And to those fans, she never let any personal problems dim her screen glamour.

Marilyn Monroe's will is filed for probate with more than half of her $500,000 estate going to *"The Method"* acting coach, **Lee Strasberg**.

At **Marilyn Monroe's** crypt, **Joe DiMaggio** makes arrangements to keep the black vase filled with fresh red roses twice a week forever.

The star led a far from normal childhood and had twelve sets of foster parents, leaving her to say in her last interview that she was unaccustomed to being happy and it wasn't something she ever took for granted. Despite flashes of temperament and tantrums, she turned in performances that kept her among the greatest box office favorites in motion picture history.

1962

PRESIDENT KENNEDY RECEIVES HONORARY DEGREE FROM YALE UNIVERSITY

2,000 people attend graduation ceremonies on Yale University's old campus.

President Kennedy and Dean Acheson (center) have been invited to receive honorary degrees.

The President, a Harvard graduate, is made an honorary Doctor of Laws before delivering the commencement address.

He takes the occasion to call on business and labor to cooperate with the government in furthering the nation's economic growth. However, he begins on a lighter note. "It might be said now, that I have the best of both worlds—a Harvard education and a Yale degree. I am particularly glad to become a Yale man because as I think about my troubles I find that a lot of them have come from other Yale men."

28

Kennedy

THE KENNEDY CHARISMA FACTOR

At the annual Press Week gathering in New York publishers agree that President Kennedy is at the height of his popularity, citing his handling of the steel crisis and his foreign policy program as well as his personal charisma and his family life.

When asked to comment on the press treatment of his administration, President Kennedy remarks: *"Well, I'm reading it more and enjoying it less."*

HE'S IN THE MONEY!

JFK becomes the richest president in U.S. history when he receives another fourth of his share in three trusts established by his father, Joseph P. Kennedy, bringing JFK's share to $10 million.

The President purchases a 39-acre piece of property near Middleburg, Virginia and plans to build a ranch-style home on it.

The President and the First Lady visit Mexico City on their first trip to Mexico.

WHAT A HUNK!

President Kennedy is mobbed by hundreds of swooning bathers as he takes a dip in the ocean in Santa Monica.

JAZZIN' UP The WHITE HOUSE

A jazz concert is performed for the first time at the White House featuring The Paul Winter Jazz Sextet in the stately East Room.

WHAT A YEAR IT WAS!

Korner

Jackie reiterates her annoyance at having her children stalked by photographers in a mail interview by an Associated Press reporter.

Jackie visits Rome and is entertained by the Italian president and his wife and has an audience with Pope John XXIII.

Jackie lunches with Queen Elizabeth II at Buckingham Palace.

In Pakistan, Jackie is presented with a riding horse from President Mohammed Ayub Khan and visits the historic Khyber Pass.

In Groton, Connecticut Jackie christens "Lafayette," the world's largest submarine.

Jackie guides millions of television viewers on a tour of the White House in an hour-long program aired simultaneously by NBC, ABC and CBS.

JUST MOM & ME

Caroline Kennedy and her mom watch Moscow's Bolshoi Ballet rehearse for their evening show at Washington's Capital Theater.

Miss Porter's School in Farmington, Connecticut receives an application from Jackie Kennedy on behalf of her four-year-old daughter Caroline for admission to the school in about ten years. Tuition, room and board: $2,750.

President and Mrs. Kennedy play host to 49 Nobel Laureates at the White House with JFK saying: *"I think this is the most extraordinary collection of talent, of human knowledge, that has ever been gathered together at the White House— with the possible exception of when Thomas Jefferson dined alone."*

WHAT A YEAR IT WAS!

1962

JACKIE VISITS INDIA

Before leaving India for her visit to Pakistan, the First Lady decides to have a ride on an 8-foot elephant decked out in all of his royal trappings. Accompanied by her sister Princess Radziwill, Jackie begins her 10-minute ride aboard Bebia or baby.

The Mahout explains that he and the elephant grew up together and they are both 35.

Mrs. Kennedy calls this one of the most delightful interludes on her visit to India.

29

IT'S A CRIME

Attorney General Robert F. Kennedy goes on an informal goodwill tour of the world.

100,000 West Berliners line the streets in a bitter cold snowstorm to welcome **Bobby** and **Ethel Kennedy**.

MAKING A BIG SPLASH

Throwing a bash at her home, white-gowned **Ethel Kennedy** falls into the swimming pool along with two other guests.

Edward Kennedy admits being thrown out of Harvard for cheating on exams.

Marilyn Monroe dazzles a crowd of 15,000 gathered at Madison Square Garden to honor President Kennedy's 45th birthday when she sings "Happy birthday dear Mr. President" swathed in a skintight, flesh-tone gown.

HELL NO, HE WON'T JOIN

President Kennedy withdraws his application to join the exclusive Cosmos Club of Washington, D.C. after the club refuses membership to a black U.S. Department of State official.

The White House's private nursery and kindergarten attended by **Caroline Kennedy** becomes integrated when black Presidential press aide **Andrew T. Hatcher's** five-year-old son joins the class of 20.

Ex-Tito aide Milovan Djilas is arrested in Belgrade for his book on Stalin.

SPY NO MORE

Convicted Russian spy **Robert A. Soblen** flees to Tel Aviv, Israel to avoid going to prison for wartime espionage against the U.S. and commits suicide in London where he was awaiting deportation to America to serve his prison sentence.

The U.S. indicts Teamster Jimmy Hoffa for accepting $1 million illegally from a Detroit trucking line.

In Texas, Billie Sol Estes is found guilty of a real estate swindle.

A Texas court declares controversial land financier Billie Sol Estes bankrupt.

HE'S JUST HORSING AROUND

Walter Winchell does an impromptu interview with racketeer **Frank Costello** at New York's posh Stork Club during which **Costello** reveals that he's been married to the same girl for almost 40 years and that his $27,000 fine for income tax invasion is about the same amount of money he would bet on a horse.

IT COULD BE WORSE— THE RUSSIAN GULAG, LET'S SAY

Stripped of his citizenship by a U.S. district judge in 1959, **Frank Costello** loses his attempt to reverse the deportation order which will send him back to his native Italy.

Frank Costello

To each his own clean Dixie Cup! Here's a fresh idea! Replace your old bathroom glass that could spread the "bug" that lays the whole family low with a brand new, transparent Dixie Cup Dispenser. See if your family doesn't have far fewer colds this year. Goes with any color scheme. Refills available everywhere.

To each his own clean
DIXIE® CUP
PRODUCT OF AMERICAN CAN COMPANY

31

1962

Actress **Jayne Mansfield** and her husband **Mickey Hargitay** survive a harrowing night after being marooned on a small coral island six miles from Nassau in the Bahamas.

Milton Berle administers mouth-to-mouth resuscitation for 20 minutes to a man stricken with a heart attack at Las Vegas' Sands Hotel and saves his life.

Comedian **Danny Thomas** visits his ancestral site in Lebanon.

OH YE OF TOO TOO SOLID SEXY FLESH

French sex kitten **Brigitte Bardot** awakes in a hotel room in Fiesole, Italy and discovers poet **Domenico Buono** kneeling at her bedside and reciting poetry at which point she screams and has him arrested.

WE LOVE YOU FRANKIE SAN

Women scream and cameras click away as Frank Sinatra touches down at Tokyo International Airport on the first leg of his two-month tour to raise money for children's charities.

FRANKLY FRANK

Dancer Juliet Prowse goes home to South Africa for a visit as a Hollywood notable brought about by her engagement to and subsequent break-up with singer Frank Sinatra.

DID YOU READ THE ONE ABOUT BEGETTING & BEGATTING?

Frank is presented with a key to Nazareth, a silver-embossed Bible and attends the groundbreaking ceremonies for the Frank Sinatra International Friendship Youth House.

Frank battles with 50 neighbors over his right to establish a private heliport outside his home in the Coldwater Canyon section of Beverly Hills.

"SET 'EM UP JOE," AT BING'S HOUSE

Frank is terribly angry when on a visit to California President Kennedy opts to stay at Bing Crosby's house in Palm Springs instead of the new "Presidential Wing" Frank built just for JFK and retaliates by eliminating the president's brother-in-law, Peter Lawford, from his luncheon list.

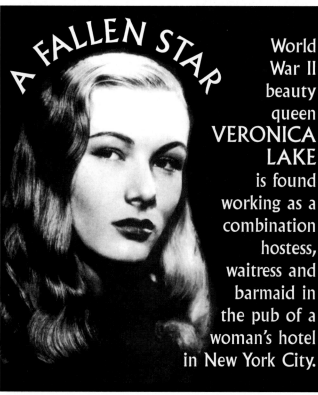

A FALLEN STAR

World War II beauty queen **VERONICA LAKE** is found working as a combination hostess, waitress and barmaid in the pub of a woman's hotel in New York City.

She's Dreaming Of A Wet Christmas

BING CROSBY'S only daughter, 2 1/2-year-old **Mary Frances**, becomes the youngest swimmer to earn a Red Cross beginner's certificate.

WHAT A YEAR IT WAS!

1962

Debbie Reynolds, Sammy Davis, Jr., Jayne Mansfield and super-clown Emmett Kelly are among the celebrities who entertain at a benefit for emotionally disturbed children.

Actor Mickey Rooney files for bankruptcy in Los Angeles Federal Court.

Imitating the antics of Elizabeth Taylor and Richard Burton, Mike Nichols and model Suzy Parker in cahoots with photographer Richard Avedon stage a brawl in a Paris nightclub to garner publicity for gorgeous new Paris fashions.

MY FAIR LADY'S Julie Andrews gives birth to little Emma.

IF YOU KNEW SWOOSIE, YOU'D KNOW SHE'S A DOOSIE

17-year-old Swoosie Kurtz, daughter of pilot Frank Kurtz, who flew the second most famous bomber in World War II called the SWOOSE (A-bomber ENOLA GAY is #1), enters University of Southern California to study drama.

Tom Brokaw graduates from the University of South Dakota and begins his career in journalism.

SAY THE MAGIC WOID AND WE'LL KICK YOU AROUND AGAIN

With **Groucho Marx** for a neighbor, **Richard Nixon** moves into his $135,000 Beverly Hills home replete with three fireplaces, four bedrooms, six baths and a swimming pool.

THE LITTLE TRAMP GOES TO COLLEGE

Oxford University honors 73-year-old Englishman **Charlie Chaplin** with a Doctor of Letters degree for the pleasure he has given people over the years.

AND AWAY WEEEEE GO ON THE CHOO CHOO

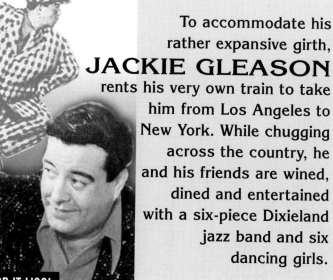

To accommodate his rather expansive girth, **JACKIE GLEASON** rents his very own train to take him from Los Angeles to New York. While chugging across the country, he and his friends are wined, dined and entertained with a six-piece Dixieland jazz band and six dancing girls.

Elvis Presley gets a visit from **Priscilla Beaulieu** who flies from West Germany to visit him over Christmas.

WHAT A YEAR IT WAS!

1962

Research nutritionist Beatrice Finkelstein packs Astronaut John H. Glenn, Jr.'s lunch box for his three-orbit journey into outer space which includes squeeze tubes of beef, vegetables and applesauce.

HAIL THE SPACE CONQUERING HERO

In Washington D.C., tens of thousands of people turn out in the rain to honor **John H. Glenn, Jr.**, the first American to orbit the earth.

Dumping more confetti than the city has seen since the end of World War II, John H. Glenn, Jr. gets a tumultuous welcome in New York City.

John Glenn's orbital flight is the most emotionally gripping news story of the year as the nation stays glued to television sets for the 12 hours of coverage.

LET ME TELL YOU ABOUT MY SON THE ASTRONAUT

John H. Glenn, Jr.'s mom, Mrs. John H. Glenn, Sr., is chosen World Mother of the Year.

America's newest hero, John H. Glenn, Jr., is chosen Father of the Year by the National Father's Day Committee.

STILL FLYING HIGH

The seven Mercury astronauts – John Glenn, Scott Carpenter, Walter Schirra, Alan Shepard, Virgil Grissom, Leroy Cooper and Donald Slayton – visit the new $90 million Manned Spacecraft Center in Houston, Texas.

JUST A HEARTBEAT AWAY

NASA announces that due to an erratic heartbeat, Donald "Deke" Slayton will no longer be eligible for a solo ride into space and is being reassigned to ground duties.

BUT OFFICER, NO ONE GAVE ME A TICKET FOR GOING 5,000 MPH

Astronaut **Virgil Grissom** is ticketed in Florida for doing 70 in a 55 zone and when he fails to pay the fine, a warrant is issued for his arrest prompting NASA to quickly send a money order.

The following are on **EBONY** magazine's list of the wealthiest blacks in America:

Adam Clayton Powell, Jr. (Congressman)

Eddie "Rochester" Anderson (Comedian)

Floyd Patterson (Heavyweight Champ)

Jackie Robinson (Baseball Hall of Famer)

Marian Anderson (Singer)

Harry Belafonte (Singer)

Nat "King" Cole (Singer)

Lena Horne (Singer)

Johnny Mathis (Singer)

Cole

Belafonte

After eight months of dilly-dallying by southern senators, the nomination of black leader Thurgood Marshall as a Federal circuit judge is approved by the Senate Judiciary Committee.

NOT A BAGEL OR CHICKEN WING IN THE HOUSE

NEW YORK'S MAYOR ROBERT F. WAGNER gives up his membership at the New York Athletic Club citing the club's discriminatory practices in barring blacks and Jews.

WHAT A YEAR IT WAS!

GENERAL HOSPITAL

In Nevada to divorce her third husband, film producer **Sid Luft**, **Judy Garland** gets emergency treatment for what is described by doctors as *"an acute kidney ailment,"* not an overdose of barbiturates.

+ In Washington, Supreme Court Justice **Felix Frankfurter** is hospitalized after collapsing from an interruption of blood flow to the brain.

+ Actor **Van Johnson** severs his finger at the first joint during the filming of the opening scene of *The Music Man*. It is later stitched back onto his hand at Charing Cross Hospital.

+ **Bing Crosby** is resting in a Santa Monica hospital after his third kidney stone operation.

+ Ambassador to India **John Kenneth Galbraith** is hospitalized with an intestinal disorder.

+ While vacationing at Monte Carlo's Hotel de Paris, 87-year-old former Prime Minister **Sir Winston Churchill** slips and falls as he gets out of bed sustaining a snapped bone in his left thigh.

+ **Jackie Gleason** undergoes surgery for a lump in his neck.

+ **Herbert Hoover** recuperates from surgery to remove a tumor.

Edward G. Robinson suffers a heart attack while on location in the foothills of Tanganyika's Mount Kilimanjaro.

Stroke victim JOSEPH P. KENNEDY is flown to Manhattan's Institute of Physical Medicine and Rehabilitation for treatment.

ROSE FITZGERALD KENNEDY undergoes surgery to correct a pelvic hernia.

UP IN FLAMES

Pop singer **Brenda Lee** is slightly injured after running into her burning home in Nashville to try to save her dog Cee Cee who later dies of smoke inhalation.

1962

ON THE DOMESTIC FRONT

Miffed that a Santa Monica judge grants her ex-husband **Marlon Brando** additional visitation with their 3-year-old son **Christian Devi, Anna Kashfi** hauls off and slugs him outside the courtroom.

At his request, **Mrs. Mary Todhunter Clark Rockefeller** grants her husband, New York's Governor **Nelson Rockefeller**, a Reno divorce.

Sophia Loren has her marriage to **Carlo Ponti** annulled to save him from bigamy charges.

The Story Of Liz, Ed, Dick & Sybil

Elizabeth Taylor and her husband **Eddie Fisher** adopt a one-year-old orphan.

Crooner Eddie Fisher, rested after spending a few days in a private psychiatric hospital in Manhattan, denies there is anything going on between his wife, Elizabeth Taylor, and her *Cleopatra* co-star, **Richard Burton**. Fisher laughs off rumors of his nervous breakdown and possible break-up of his marriage. The "unromantically involved" *Cleopatra* screen couple are later seen in Rome dancing and kissing.

Richard Burton has a rendezvous with his wife **Sybil** in Paris where they picnic with their children.

Elizabeth Taylor is rushed to a hospital in Rome with a case of food poisoning and refuses to see her husband Eddie who flies in from Portugal to be at his wife's side. He is allowed to escort her home the next day.

Elizabeth issues instructions to her attorney to terminate the services of her fourth husband, Eddie Fisher.

Elizabeth and Richard have a spat in a Rome nightclub.

Elizabeth and Richard arrive in London to begin filming *The V.I.P.s*.

WHAT A YEAR IT WAS!

an
American
tradition...

the family Frigidaire refrigerator

fashion-fresh and full of features for 1963

More people own Frigidaire refrigerators than any other kind. It's an American tradition—the family Frigidaire refrigerator. ▪ Look at the big, beautiful 1963 Frigidaire refrigerators some day soon. They come in all sizes and prices to fit big and little families and pocketbooks. Admire their sleek fashion-fresh lines and colors. Marvel at the miracle of a Frost-Proof model, with a right temperature for everything from meat to butter, that's as clear of frost as a day in June. Delight in the quick flip that sends ice cubes cascading into the built-in ice bin. Roll out the shelves, peek in all the compartments, discover the exactly perfect place and space for everything from eggs to bottles tall and small. Above all, note that Frigidaire quality. Every Frigidaire refrigerator has it. ▪ You'll see right away why so many people say "there's just no substitute for the real thing—the original Frigidaire refrigerator."

Features mentioned above are standard on Model shown. (FPI-16B-63)

FRIGIDAIRE

37

1962

Coupling

Frankie Avalon & Kay Diebel

Piper Laurie & Joseph Morgenstern

Jack Lemmon & Felicia Farr

Placido Domingo & Marta Ornelas

Janet Leigh & Robert Brandt

Andy Williams & Claudine Longet

Rex Harrison & Rachel Roberts

John Hurt & Annette Robertson

Sean Connery & Diane Cilento

Christopher Plummer & Patricia Lewis

Deborah Kerr & Peter Viertel

Jon Voight & Lauri Peters

Anna Mae "Tina" Bullock & Ike Turner

Lee Grant & Joseph Feury

Tom Brokaw & Meredith Auld

Dick Clark & Loretta Martin

Linda Christian & Edmund Purdom

Tony Richardson & Vanessa Redgrave

Edith Piaf & Theo Sarapo

Mary Tyler Moore & Grant Tinker

Zeppo Marx & Barbara Blakeley

Ed "Kookie" Byrnes & Asa Maynor

Nancy Kwan & Peter Pock

Zsa Zsa Gabor & Herbert Loeb Hutner

Elizabeth Ashley & James Farentino

Olympia Dukakis & Louis Zorich

Uncoupling

Lana Turner **&** Fred May

Dinah Shore **&** George Montgomery

Brigitte Bardot **&** Jacques Charrier

Michael Landon **&** Dodie Frasier Landon

Carol Burnett **&** Don Saroyan

Dorothy Dandridge **&** Jack Denison

Robert Wagner **&** Natalie Wood

Eric Sevareid **&** Lois Finger Sevareid

Cary Grant **&** Betsy Drake

Tony Curtis **&** Janet Leigh

Ginger Rogers **&** William Marshall

Dean Stockwell **&** Millie Perkins

Woody Allen **&** Harlene Rosen

Johnny Weissmuller **&** Ailene Gates

1962

Queen Mother Elizabeth rides with 11-year-old Princess Anne to the horse guards parade area.

The Queen salutes as she watches this impressive ceremony.

Then the Queen leads her troops back to Buckingham Palace, where she will take a final salute.

Resplendent in a tri-cornered hat and tunic granted with the Order of the Garter, Queen Elizabeth rides forth to take the salute at the annual Trooping of the Colors, a ritual marking the ninth anniversary of her coronation. Though born in April, today is considered Queen Elizabeth's official birthday so it's a dual celebration of both the coronation and her birthday.

At the Palace, the royal family watches from the balcony as the impressive ceremony nears its climax.

QUEEN ELIZABETH
CELEBRATES NINTH ANNIVERSARY OF HER CORONATION

Loyal subjects line up to watch the festivities and get a glimpse of their Queen.

40

WHAT A YEAR IT WAS!

The 250-year-old ceremony has remained unchanged through the centuries. A symbol of patriotism and deference to the Crown.

The Queen receives a tribute to her rule as a beloved monarch.

A ROYAL PAIN IN THE STOMACH

13-year-old **Prince Charles** is rushed from Cheam School by ambulance to London's Hospital for Sick Children with acute appendicitis.

According to the Headmaster of Gordonstoun in Scotland, the 13-year-old Prince of Wales is near the top of his class of 28, where cold showers and running kick off each day at **Prince Philip's** alma mater.

GETTING INTO FOCUS

Princess Margaret's husband, **Earl of Snowdon**, formerly **Antony Armstrong-Jones**, shoots his first photographs for Britain's *Sunday Times*.

Queen Elizabeth attends a film preview of *West Side Story* and meets actor **Yul Brynner** who is part of a Hollywood delegation attending the premiere.

THE DUCHESS DOES THE SUPERMARKETS— A TALE OF ROYAL TASTES

The **Duchess of Windsor** reveals that one of her favorite things to do in America is to go shopping in a supermarket for products that are hard to find in England such as angel food mix, corn muffin mix, canned corn, canned black cherries and Blue Cheer detergent.

LET'S TWIST AGAIN BUT OH MY ACHING EVERYTHING

After taking a quick lesson from an American fashion model, the 67-year-old **Duke of Windsor** struts his stuff and does The Twist at a Paris ball.

The Duke and Duchess of Windsor spend their silver wedding anniversary sailing to Europe on the liner *United States*.

SHE'S MUM ABOUT WHETHER SHE'S GOING TO BE A MUM AGAIN

No confirmation is forthcoming from the Palace with regard to articles appearing in London's newspapers speculating on whether or not **Princess Margaret** is pregnant.

The best royal catch in the world is Britain's **Prince Charles**.

1962

THE ROYALS OF THE WORLD

PRINCESS SOPHIA of Greece marries **PRINCE JUAN CARLOS** of Spain in Athens.

Jordan celebrates the birth of an heir to the throne with the arrival of **KING HUSSEIN'S** new son, **ABDULLAH**, who is named crown prince.

THE BLUE BLOOD IS FLOWING

Britain's **QUEEN ELIZABETH II**, Iran's **SHAH** and **EMPRESS FARAH**, Norway's **KING OLAV V**, Luxembourg's **GRAND DUCHESS CHARLOTTE** and **KING BAUDOUIN** of the Belgians are among the reigning monarchs who show up to celebrate the Netherlands' **QUEEN JULIANA'S** 53rd birthday and 25th wedding anniversary.

The royal family of Japan is looking for an appropriate girl from a decent home for 27-year-old **PRICE YOSHI**.

JUST HEAR THOSE SLEIGH BELLS JINGLE

Monaco's **PRINCESS GRACE** takes her two children—**PRINCESS CAROLINE** and **PRINCE ALBERT**—tobogganing in the Alps.

THE PRINCESS IS NOT HEADING NORTH BY NORTHWEST

Monaco's **PRINCESS GRACE** turns down an offer to make a Hitchcock film citing that she can't leave her husband, the Prince, and their children.

SHAH OF IRAN

The powerful Shah of Iran arrives in Washington on a three-day visit.

A devout Muslim, he begins his stay by touring a beautiful Washington mosque, a place of worship that was built with contributions from Muslims from all parts of the world.

The Shah is presented with a memento of his visit to this center of Muslim culture.

42

ISITS WASHINGTON

The White House is ablaze as the Shah and his lovely queen arrive for a state dinner.

Jackie Kennedy greets the Shah sporting a new hairdo called "brioche," as the President welcomes Queen Farah who wears a priceless tiara.

The royal visitors are treated to the first ballet ever performed in the White House. It is a gala affair.

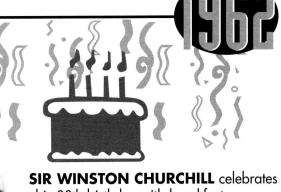

1962

SIR WINSTON CHURCHILL celebrates his 88th birthday with breakfast consisting of a soft-boiled egg followed by a glass of champagne.

Celebrating his 94th birthday, former Vice President **JOHN NANCE GARNER** announces he has to give up his last vice—smoking black stogies.

OLD SOLDIERS DO RETURN
General of the Army **DOUGLAS MACARTHUR** celebrates his 82nd birthday in New York.

Republic of China's President **CHIANG KAI-SHEK** quietly celebrates his 75th birthday at a retreat near Taipei.

THE POPE IS LOOKING POOPED AND PALE
81-year-old **Pope John XXIII** appears before 1,200 people in his first audience since recovering from anemia.

Pulitzer Prize-winning playwright of *"Our Town"* and *"The Skin of Our Teeth,"* **THORNTON WILDER** decides to give up life in the big city and opts for a more relaxed, unsophisticated way of living by moving near Tucson, Arizona for two years.

Bertrand Russell calls Atomic tests "butchery."

PASSINGS
A heart attack takes the life of Cosa Nostra boss and international racketeer **Charles "Lucky" Luciano***, age 64.*

Queen of the Netherlands for 50 years until her abdication in 1948, **Wilhelmina** *dies at age 82.*

President Kennedy appoints **Byron R. White** an Associate Justice of the Supreme Court.

U.S. Supreme Court Justice **Felix Frankfurter** retires and **Arthur J. Goldberg** receives the appointment from President Kennedy.

Anthony J. Celebrezze is the first replacement in President Kennedy's cabinet succeeding **Abraham A. Ribicoff** as Secretary of Health, Education and Welfare.

President Kennedy appoints **Cyrus R. Vance** as Secretary of the Army upon the resignation of **Elvis J. Stahr**.

General **Maxwell Taylor** succeeds General **Lauris Norstad** as head of U.S. Joint Chiefs of Staff.

THERE'S NO PLACE LIKE THE HOUSE

VICE PRESIDENT LYNDON B. JOHNSON wins admiration from members of the President's Commission on the Status of Women led by former First Lady Eleanor Roosevelt when he says: *"I believe a woman's place is not only in the home, but in the House and in the Senate."*

Vice President Lyndon B. Johnson returns to Washington after visiting six Mediterranean and Middle East nations with his wife and daughters.

As part of his 2,000-mile tour, former **President Eisenhower** and his wife **Mamie** touch down in Dublin where they are greeted with shouts of *I LIKE IKE* in Gaelic.

Dwight & Mamie Eisenhower arrive in Abilene, Kansas for dedication ceremonies of the $3 million Eisenhower Presidential Library.

TALES FROM POLICITICAL WATERS

55-year-old best-selling author **James Michener** is named the Democrat candidate for Congress from the 8th Congressional District of Pennsylvania.

Senator **Carl Hayden**, Democrat from Arizona, completes 50 years of service in the U.S. Congress, the longest in history.

Tom Hayden is elected president of Students For A Democratic Society.

For the second time in a year, an attempt is made on French President CHARLES DE GAULLE'S life as he leaves Paris for his country home at Colombey-les-deux-Eglises.

IF YOU KNEW HARRY LIKE WE KNOW HARRY
Former President **Harry S. Truman** is the subject of a roast at the Circus Saints & Sinners luncheon club in Manhattan and takes the lampooning like a good sport.

PRESIDENTS TWO
31st President of the U.S. Herbert Hoover helps the 33rd President of the U.S. Harry S. Truman dedicate his presidential library in Independence, Missouri.

44

Comedian **Bob Hope** is honored with a Congressional Gold Medal for entertaining our servicemen all over the world going back to World War II.

YOU SURE YOU GOT THE RIGHT LADY?

On receiving a medal from the Paris Post of the American Legion for furthering Franco-American relations, **Sophia Loren** says that she's quite confused as to exactly what she's done to deserve the honor and the presenter is hard-pressed to give her a satisfactory answer.

U.N. Under Secretary and Nobel Peace Prize winner **Ralph Bunche** is chosen CITIZEN OF THE YEAR by the Golden Key Council.

82-year-old General **Douglas MacArthur** receives a special resolution from the U.S. Congress thanking him for his leadership "during and following World War II" and for his efforts to strengthen the ties between the Philippines and the United States.

AND NOW, CAN YOU NAME "TWENTY-ONE" WAYS TO SAY I'M SORRY

Charles Van Doren, former professor at Columbia University, and nine other former contestants on rigged TV quiz shows, plead guilty to perjury charges and receive suspended sentences. Van Doren would like to disappear from public view and go back to teaching.

REIGNING WORLD BEAUTIES

Jackie Kennedy	(United States)
Princess Grace	(Monaco)
Queen Fabiola	(Belgium)
Queen Sirikit	(Thailand)
Maria Tereza Goulart	(Brazil)
Empress Farah Diba	(Iran)
Marie-Therese Houphouet-Boigny	(Ivory Coast's First Lady)
Toni Gardiner	(Jordan)

THERE'S NO BUSINESS LIKE THE STOCK BUSINESS

Show business entrepreneur **Billy Rose** boasts that he is the largest individual stockholder of AT&T with his 80,000 shares worth around $8.3 million.

THE LAST OF THE BIG SPENDERS

Words of wisdom from multi-millionaire Arkansas farmer **Winthrop Rockefeller** include watching the dimes so the dollars will take care of themselves and *"never overtip."*

NOBEL•PEACE•PRIZE
Linus
PAULING
USA

The U.S. Post Office issues a $.04 stamp honoring the late Dag Hammarskjold.

ARTIST **PABLO PICASSO** IS AWARDED THE LENIN PEACE PRIZE.

1962 ADVERTISEMENT

FOR THE MOST WELCOME GIFTS OF ALL...

"GIVE A CHRISTMAS GIFT FOR THE HOME"

Gifts for the home are the most satisfying gifts to give—and the most appreciated. They are useful all year long and a constant reminder of the giver's thoughtfulness. You'll find a sleighful of suggestions for "Christmas Gifts For The Home" in the November and December issues of American Home. Some of these exciting gift ideas are featured on this page. (And you can buy hundreds of other gifts direct by mail through the American Home Market Place, one of the country's favorite magazine shopping sections.)

The Hoover Portable

General Electric Housewares

Whirlpool Dishwashers

Pyrexware

Decorating Book by Armstrong Flooring

Presto Coffeemakers

Ronson Can-Do Electric Can Openers

Kroehler Furniture

American-Standard Sink Faucets

GIVE A GULISTAN CARPET

Karagheusian

Frigidaire Dishmobile

LONGINES
The World's Most Honored Watch

Health-O-Meter by Continental Scales

The Gorham Company

Barcalo

Congoleum-Nairn
FINE FLOORS

Congoleum-Nairn

WELDWOOD
Real Wood Paneling

Weldwood

Ronson Lighters

Frigidaire Automatic Washers

GIVE A CHRISTMAS GIFT FOR THE HOME

FINE STORES THROUGHOUT THE COUNTRY FEATURING THE THEME "GIVE A CHRISTMAS GIFT FOR THE HOME" INCLUDE POLK BROTHERS, CHICAGO...GIMBELS NEW YORK...BREUNER'S, NORTHERN CALIFORNIA... SCRUGGS-VANDERVOORT-BARNEY, INC., ST. LOUIS... AND BULLOCK'S DOWNTOWN, LOS ANGELES.

AMERICAN HOME

HUMAN INTEREST

AND THEN THERE WERE FIVE

Two members of the **FLYING WALLENDAS'** high-wire act are killed when their seven-man pyramid collapses during a performance in Detroit.

HARDLY A WHISPER

Thanks to First Lady Jackie Kennedy and screen star Marilyn Monroe, women from the "smart set" are speaking in tiny little voices.

TYING HIS LAST KNOT

Albert DeSalvo, "THE BOSTON STRANGLER" whose signature is a bow tied on his victim, is finally caught but not before committing a string of grotesquely violent rapes and murders of mostly elderly women.

SWING YOUR PARTNER LEFT & THEN SWING YOUR PARTNER RIGHT

More than 8,000 square dancers arrive in Oakland for the ninth annual Golden State Roundup.

HOORAY FOR MICKEY-SAN!

Tourists from France, Britain, Germany and Japan name *Disneyland* the No. 1 tourist attraction in the U.S.

AMERICAN MOTHER OF THE YEAR

Mrs. Mary Celesta Weatherly
De Kalb County, Alabama

MISS UNIVERSE

Argentina's beautiful 24-year-old
Norma Beatriz Nolan

WHAT A YEAR IT WAS!

47

JUST THE FACTS

The world population is over **three billion**.

Average Life Expectancy In The U.S. **70 Years**

It is estimated that by the year 2000,10% of the U.S. population will be made up of people over 65.

With a U.S. population of over 188,000,000, New York and California are neck in neck for the #1 position of the most populated state in the Union.

According to the U.N. Educational, Scientific & Cultural Organization, 44% of the world's population is illiterate.

More U.S. families own television sets than telephones according to the U.S. Census Bureau.

According to Max Jaeger, President of the Food Service Executives Association, Inc., home cooking will soon be a thing of the past as 37% of the food eaten in the U.S. is already being prepared by professionals.

An unsettling report appears in the **Journal of the American Medical Association** indicating that more children die from parental beatings than diseases such as leukemia, cystic fibrosis and muscular dystrophy.

WATCH YOUR STEP, PLEASE
Falls are found to be the leading cause of accidents, accounting for around 27% of all injuries.

YOU'VE HEARD OF THE CITY OF LIGHTS? WELL, HERE'S THE CITY OF BAGELS, STEW, PIZZA AND TACOS
New census figures indicate that in addition to boasting more Jews than Tel Aviv, as many Irish and Italians as Dublin and Rome respectively, New York City now has more Puerto Ricans than San Juan.

ENOUGH TO MAKE YOU CHOKE ON YOUR STEAK
According to Dr. Norman C. Wright, deputy director of the U.N. Food and Agriculture Organization, one-third to one-half of the world suffers from chronic hunger or malnutrition.

LEO WITH A MOON IN PISCES
Approximately 5,000 people in the U.S. earn their income as full-time astrologers with around 100,000 dabbling part-time. Total earnings are estimated at $100 million a year.

According to the American Kennel Club, poodles hold first place in total number of registrations with beagles, chihuahuas, dachshunds and German shepherds next in the barking order.

THE STORKS ARE FLYING OVERTIME
Somewhere in the world, three babies are born every second with almost two million born in one week.

THE MIGHTIEST GIRTH OF ALL
Oregon wins the prize for the tree with the largest girth with its Clatsop fir measuring 15.48 feet residing near Seaside, Oregon.

CALIFORNIA HERE THEY COME
From all over America, more than 1,000 people a day arrive in the land of palm trees, surfboards and flowing blond tresses.

WE'RE ON THE ROAD AGAIN
One out of five Americans moves annually collectively spending around $1 billion on associated costs.

WHAT A YEAR IT WAS!

ADOLF EICHMANN is hanged in Israel's Ramle prison for crimes against the Jewish people, crimes against humanity and other war crimes.

Bronx police seize $20 million worth of heroin.

The Federal Bureau of Narcotics reports a large reduction in drug addiction with only one addict in every 4,000 people.

NOW WAS THAT A TEASPOON OR A TABLESPOON?
Using spoons, Frank L. Morris, John Anglin and Clarence Anglin dig their way out of Alcatraz.

GOOD TRY, NOW BACK TO SOLITARY
Bank robber John Paul Scott is the first man to escape from Alcatraz and swim to the mainland but alas despite a valiant effort, is picked up by authorities and returned to the prison.

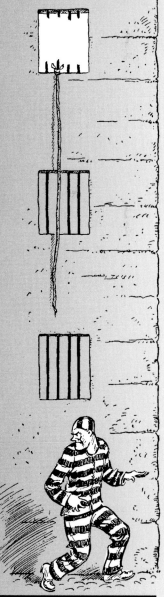

NEW YORK CITY'S FINEST Act As Coy Decoys

Select policemen, members of the Tactical Patrol Force, dress up in ladies' clothing and patrol New York's parks and streets in a campaign to catch muggers.

Belgium acquits five in euthanasia of thalidomide baby.

In the largest amount ever paid in a pollution case, The Glen Alden Mining Co. pays the Pennsylvania State Justice Department $45,000 for polluting the Susquehanna River and killing over 115,000 fish.

THE CASH WAS IN THE MAIL
In the largest robbery in Post Office history, enterprising bandits make off with over $1 million in cash from an unarmed truck.

THEY REALLY HIT THE NUMBERS
Workmen find over $2 million in cash hidden in the trunk of an old car in Jersey City, N.J. believed to belong to gambler Joseph Vincent "Newsboy" Moriarty, serving time for possession of policy slips.

The U.S. Supreme Court overturns contempt convictions against six people who took the Fifth Amendment in congressional loyalty inquiries.

A priceless 444-piece coin collection is stolen from the Truman Library in Independence, Missouri including a 1796 quarter valued at $4,000 and a $5 gold piece valued at $1,500.

A VERY EXPENSIVE PENNY FOR YOUR THOUGHTS?
A U.S. copper penny from 1799 sells for $10,500.

WHAT A YEAR IT WAS!

49

Ceremonies at the Lincoln Memorial mark the centennial of Emancipation Proclamation.

Jackson

Gospel singer **Mahalia Jackson** sings *The Battle Hymn of the Republic* kicking off the centennial celebration of Abraham Lincoln's Emancipation Proclamation.

Governor **Ross Barnett** defies federal court order and forbids the University of Mississippi from admitting **James Meredith**.

- - -

200 arrested in riots as **James Meredith** attends classes.

Meredith

- - -

Defying orders to desegregate Catholic churches in New Orleans, three segregationists are excommunicated by Roman Catholic **Archbishop Joseph Francis Rummel**.

- - -

New Orleans' segregationists offer blacks free one-way bus tickets to northern cities.

- - -

The worst race riot since 1910 breaks out on Thanksgiving Day at the District of Columbia Stadium during a high school championship football game.

- - -

President Kennedy denounces church burnings in Georgia.

BREAKING THE COLOR BARRIER

- Ordering the State of Mississippi to yield on integration, President Kennedy federalizes Mississippi National Guard.

- The U.S. Justice Department files first federal suit to end racial segregation in public schools.

- 33 public school districts are integrated this year for a total of 948 in 17 southern states and Washington, D.C.

- The Federal Government files suit to halt segregation in the public schools of Prince George County, Virginia.

- Rochester, New York schools are sued by the NAACP for de facto segregation.

- The U.S. Supreme Court reverses convictions of six Freedom Riders.

- With the exception of the National Guard, the Defense Department orders the racial integration of all military reserve units.

- The House passes bill for equal pay regardless of sex.

- President Kennedy bars religious or racial discrimination in federally funded housing.

AN IGLOO FOR EVERYONE
Alaska is the first state to pass legislation prohibiting discrimination in both public and private housing.

1962

Venerable JOHN M. BURGESS, former Episcopal Archdeacon of Boston, becomes the first black to serve as a bishop of white Episcopalian congregations in the U.S.

•

U.S. Navy Commander SAMUEL L. GRAVELY, JR. becomes the first black officer to command a combat ship, the "U.S.S. Falgout."

•

EDITH SAMPSON is the first black woman elected to the bench in Illinois.

•

LEROY R. JOHNSON is the first black elected to the Georgia senate in almost a century.

•

Pepsi-Cola Company promotes HARVEY C. RUSSELL to vice president, making him the first black to hold such a position in an international corporation.

King, Jr.

Reverend **Martin Luther King, Jr.** is jailed in Albany, Georgia for leading a protest march without a permit.

Trying to avoid mass demonstrations, Albany, Georgia city officials decide to release **Dr. Martin Luther King, Jr.** and the **Rev. Ralph Abernathy** after two weeks in jail.

CUBA broadcasts "Radio Free Dixie" praising black revolt in the South.

GREAT BRITAIN invokes the Commonwealth Immigration Act to keep out black immigrants.

CANADA eliminates all racially and religiously based immigration rules.

Amnesty International is created to monitor human rights.

The U.S. Labor Department sets a minimum wage of $.60 - $1.00 for migratory Mexican workers despite wide opposition.

Chavez

35-year-old **CESAR CHAVEZ** establishes the National Farm Workers Association.

STUDENTS AT UCLA vote to send $5,000 to Mississippi to buy appeal bonds for five Freedom Riders.

•

STUDENTS AT THE UNIVERSITY OF CHICAGO stage a two-week sit-in outside the president's office winning the right to argue their demand for integration of 150 university-owned apartment houses.

HUNDREDS OF COLLEGE STUDENTS FROM ALL OVER THE COUNTRY BRAVE WASHINGTON'S COLD WEATHER AND MARCH FOR PEACE OUTSIDE THE WHITE HOUSE.

New York police arrest 42 people at a Times Square peace rally.

AN EXPLOSIVE ISSUE
Led by Nobel Prize winner Linus Pauling, Ban-the-Bomb forces from 22 countries ask a federal court to issue injunctions against test explosions.

Britain's Prime Minister Harold Macmillan is booed by a mob of 300 brandishing Ban-the-Bomb signs.

Pauling

WHAT A YEAR IT WAS!

Amelia Earhart Memorial, commemorating her ill-fated flight around the world in 1937, is unveiled at the Miami International Airport which was her place of departure.

Earhart

The first three-engine, medium-range Boeing 727 rolls off the assembly line.

Charles "Chuck" Yeager, the first flyer to break the sound barrier in 1947, is named head of Aerospace Research Pilot School at California's Edwards Air Force Base, which will teach young flyers *"everything they need to know about being astronauts."*

As the clock strikes midnight, Braniff, Northeast and Northwest airlines move into their 100,000 square foot terminal building at New York International Airport at Idlewild.

U.S. Supreme Court rules that airports must compensate homeowners for noise and vibrations.

UP, UP & AWAY

The Record Setters

JACQUELINE COCHRAN flies from New Orleans to Hanover, Germany (5,120 miles) in 13 hours, 40 minutes.

MAJOR ROBERT M. WHITE, USAF, pilots the X-15 to an altitude of 314,750 feet and becomes the world's highest and fastest winged aircraft pilot.

NASA pilot JOSEPH A. WALKER flies the X-15 more than 4,100 mph.

And The Winners Are...

Bendix Trophy

USAF receives trophy for speed run by B-58 which flies roundtrip from Los Angeles to New York in 4 hours, 42 minutes piloted by CAPTAINS ROBERT G. SOWERS, ROBERT MACDONALD and JOHN T. WALTON.

FEDERATION AERONAUTIQUE INTERNATIONALE

De La Vaulx Medal
ASTRONAUT ALAN B. SHEPARD
LT. COL. R.G. ROBINSON (U.S. MARINES)

OCTAVE CHANUTE AWARD
NEIL A. ARMSTRONG
X-15 pilot for NASA

12th ALL WOMEN'S INTERNATIONAL AIR RACE
AILEEN SAUNDERS (El Cajon, California)

16th ANNUAL ALL-WOMEN'S TRANCONTINENTAL AIR RACE
FRANCES BERA (Pilot)
EDNA BOWEN (Co-Pilot)

HARMON INTERNATIONAL AVIATION TROPHY
PRESIDENT KENNEDY presents cosmetics company owner JACQUELINE COCHRAN her sixth Harmon trophy for racking up more individual flight records than any other pilot.

The Smithsonian is the new home of **John Glenn's** *Friendship 7* where it will be displayed along with two other great crafts – the **Wright Brothers'** *Kitty Hawk* and **Charles Lindbergh's** *Spirit of St. Louis.*

Lindbergh

Becoming the first stamp issued on the date it commemorates, a U.S. stamp of the *Mercury* space-ship is placed on sale immediately upon John Glenn's return.

THE PRINCE SPACES OUT
Thailand's **Crown Prince Vajiralongkorn** is among the 80,000 people who visit John Glenn's *Friendship 7* space capsule on display in a Bangkok park.

NASA'S DISTINGUISHED SERVICE MEDAL
Commander Petersen Walker
Major Bob White
John H. Glenn, Jr.
Scott Carpenter
Walter M. Schirra, Jr.
Walter C. Williams
Robert C. Gilruth

ONE BANANA-FLAVORED PELLET TOO MANY?
Enos, the chimpanzee who was launched into space in a *Mercury* capsule before John Glenn, dies of dysentery at New Mexico's Holloman Air Force Base.

WHAT A YEAR IT WAS!

UNDER THESE
PINK & PRETTY
SALLY VICTOR PETALS...

...IS THAT MARVELOUS NEW
GENERAL ELECTRIC PORTABLE HAIR DRYER

Lovely, isn't it! And aren't you! Because famed hat designer Sally Victor
beautifies the bonnet of the most practical hair dryer you can buy. Portable,
it travels in a pink hatbox. Lifts out and straps on, so you're free to move
about and do chores while being dried quickly, quietly, evenly . . . *com-
fortably!* It has four heats including a Cool. Use the new larger rollers?
Bonnet's supersized, covers *all!* Free offer of initials for case.
For the hair beauty you want in the time you have, and a heavenly
gift. General Electric Co., Clock & Timer Dept., Ashland, Mass.

Accent
on
VALUE

Progress Is Our Most Important Product

GENERAL ⊕ ELECTRIC

53

1962

PUTTING A NEW SPIN ON
SPIN-THE-BOTTLE

Los Angeles pre-teenagers develop a new way of "making out" with an updated version of post office and spin-the-bottle called "Seven Minutes of Heaven (or Hell)" where the boy takes the girl who is "it" into another room and can either kiss her (Heaven) or hit her (Hell) for seven minutes.

GROWN-UPS
NEED NOT APPLY

Teenage night clubs serving Coca-Cola on the rocks and pizza are springing up all over the country with names like the PEPPERMINT STICK NIGHTCLUB and CINNAMON CINDER in Los Angeles, SOC-HOP in Kansas City, THE SURF, outside of Boston, CAFÉ BIZARRE, Greenwich Village and FICKLE PICKLE in Chicago.

Naming NAMES

POPULAR NAMES

Kevin
Sean
Colin
Brian
Keith
Lynn
Jackie
Caroline
John Fitzgerald

NEW SPELLINGS

Annie
Annya
Lori
Cari
Billye
Sheryl
Cherol
Sheril

NEW DOUBLE-NAMES

Jo-Anne
Cynthia-Sue
Linda-Marie
Shirley-Lou
Mary-Lee

One out of every two first-time brides in the U.S. is a teenager.

Maybe Stick With Just "Making Out" For A While

People who marry in their teens are five times more likely to divorce than those who postpone nuptials until their 20's.

In Search Of An M.R.S. Degree

Societal pressures to marry, coupled with a young woman's drive to marry, result in the average American college girl being driven to find a husband. *Solution?* Get married first, have babies and then go to college in your 30's.

A recent Gallup poll reveals that 96% of the women who responded are happy being housewives.

ARE THERE ANY DOCTORS IN THE HOUSE (OR EVEN DENTISTS)

Singles flock to Grossinger's Hotel in the Catskills which hosts the first singles-only weekend.

54

WHAT A YEAR IT WAS!

LYNDA BIRD READY TO LEAVE THE NEST

Vice President **Lyndon B. Johnson** *speaks at his daughter's graduation from Washington's National Cathedral School for girls.*

President Kennedy *urges the nation's young people to stay in school so that they can live full, productive lives.*

JR. JR. KINDERGARTENERS

Warren, Pennsylvania decides that age five is not the only age to start school and says it will enroll bright little ones starting at three years and eight months.

A weekend in New York and a $1,000 prize goes to **Michael Day**, 14, of Hardin, Illinois and **Nettie Crawford**, 13, of Roswell, New Mexico for both winning the National Spelling Bee by successfully spelling *esquamulose*.

PHYSICAL UNFITNESS OF OUR KIDS IN PUBLIC SCHOOLS

Bud Wilkinson, Special Consultant to the President on Youth Fitness, is dismayed that 60% of our children do not exercise daily, with 26% of boys and 23% of girls unable to do pull-ups, sit-ups or squat-thrusts.

State Farm Mutual Insurance Company, the biggest auto insurer in the U.S., is going to reward 16-25-year-old males who get good grades by cutting car premiums by up to $100 if they rank in the top 20% of their classes, have B averages or prove equivalent academic standing. Girls do not have to pay extra premiums because they are considered safer drivers.

HER NUMBERS ADDED UP

Marjorie L. French, Topeka Kansas high school math teacher, is named Teacher of the Year.

HELL NO, THEY WON'T TEACH

Crippling the nation's largest urban school system, 40,000 public school teachers go on the biggest strike by public servants in U.S. history.

THIS IS A JOKING MATTER

Spider-Man debuts in *AMAZING FANTASY COMICS* No. 15.

Charles Schultz brings us *"HAPPINESS IS A WARM PUPPY."*

The National Cartoonists Society names **PEANUTS** Best Humor Strip of the Year and **William "Bill" Henry Mauldin**, soldier cartoonist of World War II fame, Cartoonist of the Year.

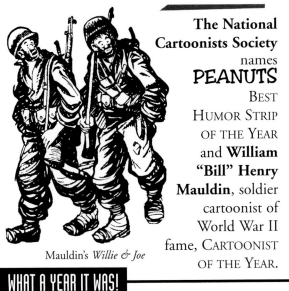

Mauldin's *Willie & Joe*

THE LOS ANGELES TIMES and Washington D.C.'s POST AND TIMES HERALD announce plans to form the first new U.S. news service since World War II.

NEWS FLASHES:

- **U.S. News & World Report** sells all its stock in the magazine to its employees.
- **LOS ANGELES EXAMINER** merges with the **HERALD-EXPRESS.**
- **LOS ANGELES MIRROR** stops rolling its presses.
- An estimated 5,700,000 readers are without their morning papers as the largest New York dailies are hit by strikes.
- After residing in Europe for the past fourteen years, syndicated columnist **Art Buchwald** is coming home to America and will settle in Washington, D.C.

WHAT A YEAR IT WAS!

1962

The Pentagon announces first federal construction plans for fallout shelters.

A ROOM AT THE INN

New York gets 13 new hotels this year.

U.S. REVERSES "CONTINENTAL DRIFT"

The construction of the Panama Canal's **Maurice H. Thatcher Ferry Bridge** will rejoin North and South America separated by the Army Corps of Engineers when the construction of the Panama Canal was completed in 1914.

- Spanning the Hudson River, the second deck of the **George Washington Bridge** opens in New York City becoming the world's only 14-lane vehicular crossing.

- Taking 12 years to build and stretching from the Atlantic to the Pacific, the **Trans-Canada Highway** opens at Roger's Pass in the Rockies.

- **The Dan Ryan Expressway**, the world's widest freeway, opens in Chicago.

- Voters in San Francisco approve tax of $792 million to pay for a 75-mile rapid transit system.

- French and Italian workers join midway under Mont Blanc marking the completion of the boring of the longest vehicular tunnel in the world scheduled for completion in the Spring of 1964.

THE NEWEST THING IN CHOO-CHOOS

The first train operating without conductors or motormen is introduced in New York City.

The world's first nuclear-powered ship, the U.S.S. Savannah, completes her maiden voyage from Yorktown, Virginia to Savannah, Georgia.

WHAT A YEAR IT WAS!

THEY CAN SEE THE FOREST AND THE TREES

The first World Conference on National Parks meets in Seattle with delegates and observers from 72 nations attending.

Passing through Utah, Colorado, New Mexico and Arizona, the last link to the famous Navajo Trail is completed.

NATIONAL PARK SERVICE HISTORIC EXPANSION *(Authorized by Congress)*

NATIONAL MONUMENT
Abraham Lincoln's boyhood home in Pigeon Creek, Indiana.

NATIONAL SEASHORES
Padre Island, Texas
Point Reyes, California

NATIONAL HISTORIC SITES
Theodore Roosevelt's home at Sagamore Hill, Long Island, N.Y. and birthplace in New York City.

CLIMB EVERY MOUNTAIN

Four British climbers, joined by four Russians, scale the highest mountain in Russia, the 24,590-foot Mount Communism.

The southeast face of Alaska's Mount McKinley is climbed for the first time.

IN SWITZERLAND, Hilti von Allmen and Walter Etter become the first to climb the north face of the Matterhorn in the winter.

ZERMATT
MATTERHORN 4505m SCHWEIZ

DON'T FORGET TO PACK YOUR "GOTGIS"

During the dog-day summer months, more than three million people flee to the Catskill Mountains, home to some 500 hotels and 800 bungalow colonies ranging from the exclusive Grossinger's and Concord hotels to *kochaleins* where family groups cook their meals in large communal kitchens.

THE DING AND THE DONG OF IT ALL

Philadelphia's Liberty Bell 209-year-old is getting a "face lift" to give it much-needed support.

Near the French-Italian border young French geologist **Michel Siffre** spends two months in a cave 400 feet underground.

Remnants of the oldest synagogue in Europe are discovered near Rome and date back to the fourth century A.D.

1962

At the White House,

following an interview by Russian editor **Aleksei I. Adzhubei**, **President Kennedy** lunches with the editor and his wife, daughter of Premier Khrushchev.

In a light moment, President Kennedy quips: *"Last year, more Americans went to concerts than baseball games. This may be viewed as an alarming statistic, but I think that both baseball and the country will endure."*

JOHN JR. AND CAROLINE AT PLAY

The White House releases a charming photograph of **Caroline** and **John Jr.** playing in their daddy, the President's office, with daddy applauding their performance.

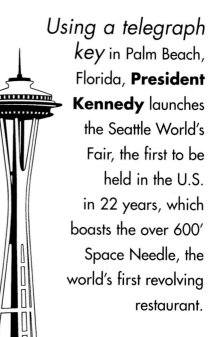

Using a telegraph key in Palm Beach, Florida, **President Kennedy** launches the Seattle World's Fair, the first to be held in the U.S. in 22 years, which boasts the over 600' Space Needle, the world's first revolving restaurant.

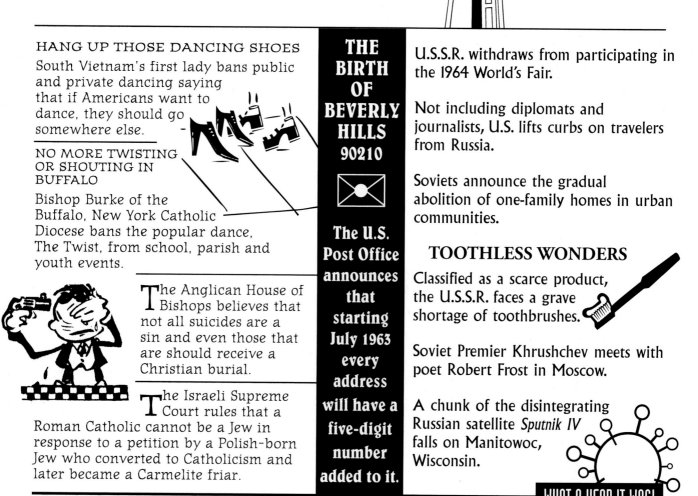

HANG UP THOSE DANCING SHOES

South Vietnam's first lady bans public and private dancing saying that if Americans want to dance, they should go somewhere else.

NO MORE TWISTING OR SHOUTING IN BUFFALO

Bishop Burke of the Buffalo, New York Catholic Diocese bans the popular dance, The Twist, from school, parish and youth events.

The Anglican House of Bishops believes that not all suicides are a sin and even those that are should receive a Christian burial.

The Israeli Supreme Court rules that a Roman Catholic cannot be a Jew in response to a petition by a Polish-born Jew who converted to Catholicism and later became a Carmelite friar.

THE BIRTH OF BEVERLY HILLS 90210

The U.S. Post Office announces that starting July 1963 every address will have a five-digit number added to it.

U.S.S.R. withdraws from participating in the 1964 World's Fair.

Not including diplomats and journalists, U.S. lifts curbs on travelers from Russia.

Soviets announce the gradual abolition of one-family homes in urban communities.

TOOTHLESS WONDERS

Classified as a scarce product, the U.S.S.R. faces a grave shortage of toothbrushes.

Soviet Premier Khrushchev meets with poet Robert Frost in Moscow.

A chunk of the disintegrating Russian satellite *Sputnik IV* falls on Manitowoc, Wisconsin.

WHAT A YEAR IT WAS!

The Coronet—world's first electric portable. Electricity makes everyone's typing look like an expert's. 5 characters repeat automatically as you hold down the key. Steel frame and jacket.

Some Santas who give fine portables look them over, type on them, check friends—and then buy Smith-Corona. Others go right out and buy Smith-Corona. For when all is said and done, more Santas buy and give Smith-Corona than any other portable! (Makes your shopping easier, doesn't it?)

(More people buy Smith-Corona than any other portable.)   SCM Corporation, 410 Park Avenue, New York 22, N. Y.

The Galaxie — world's fastest manual portable. Has a full-size office keyboard. Smart colors. Rugged steel frame and jacket. Wonderful piano-key touch. Comes with carrying case.

The Corsair—the bold new lightweight—weighs less than 10 pounds. This is the most complete low-priced portable ever. Its beautiful carrying case is actually part of the typewriter.

Thoughtful extra gift. Easiest typing course ever. On LP records. $3.95, with any new Smith-Corona portable.

1962

AUDIT

The **IRS** celebrates its 100th anniversary of relieving you of your "extra" funds.

Brooklyn's **Erasmus Hall High School**, *the nation's second oldest high school, which dates back to 1787, celebrates its 175th anniversary.*

Does Anyone Have A Chocolate Chip Cookie?

The creation of a four-cent commemorative stamp is announced by Vice President Lyndon Johnson at a luncheon celebrating the **50th year** of the **Girl Scouts of the United States of America**.

HADASSAH.

the largest Jewish woman's organization in the world, celebrates its 50th anniversary.

The 70th anniversary of Buddhism in the U.S. is celebrated.

60 YEARS OF A COLD BREEZE IN AUGUST

Air-conditioning

celebrates its 60th year of cooling us off in those hot summer months.

Getting Rid Of Those Sinking Feelings

Commemorating the 50th anniversary of the **Titanic's** sinking, 500 people attend memorial services in New York.

The U.S.S. Arizona Memorial, *a 184-foot pavilion atop the sunken battleship, is dedicated at Pearl Harbor, Hawaii.*

The American Forces Museum *opens in Sainte-Mere-Eglise, France, burial place for over 10,000 Americans, commemorating D-Day when Allied forces landed along the Normandy coast of France.*

According to a poll *of 75 men considered students of American History published in* THE NEW YORK TIMES MAGAZINE *and spearheaded by 74-year-old Emeritus Harvard Historian Arthur M. Schlesinger, Sr., following is a sampling of the ranking of American presidents:*

GREAT
Abraham Lincoln
George Washington
Franklin Delano Roosevelt
Thomas Jefferson
Woodrow Wilson

NEAR GREAT
James Polk
Harry S. Truman *(ranks 9th)*
John Adams
Grover Cleveland

AVERAGE
Dwight D. Eisenhower *(ranks 22nd)*
Andrew Johnson *(impeached)*

FAILURES
Ulysses S. Grant
Warren G. Harding

More YALE GRADUATES than HARVARD GRADUATES are listed in *WHO'S WHO* for the first time in the publication's 63-year history. *Harvard's ace in the hole?* PRESIDENT KENNEDY.

TIME MAN OF THE YEAR POPE JOHN XXIII

(first time a religious figure is the winner)

WHAT A YEAR IT WAS!

THE POPULARITY POLL

MOST ADMIRED MEN

President Kennedy *(second consecutive year)*

Former President Dwight D. Eisenhower

Sir Winston Churchill

MOST ADMIRED WOMEN

First Lady Jackie Kennedy

Queen Elizabeth II

Queen Elizabeth II

1962

Boasting a membership of over 520,000 women in 10,466 chapters in the U.S., Puerto Rico and the Virgin Islands, **Future Homemakers of America** meets in Salt Lake City, Utah.

THAT'S A LOT OF LITTLE KIWANISES

47-year-old Kiwanis Club grants the 5,000th charter to South Muncie, Indiana.

THE BERYLLIUM RUSH OF '62

Beryllium, a rare space-age metal, is discovered by U.S. geologists on the Seward Peninsula in Alaska.

THE PARTICLES WILL BE FLYING

California becomes the third state to produce asbestos.

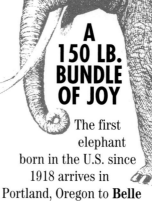

A 150 LB. BUNDLE OF JOY

The first elephant born in the U.S. since 1918 arrives in Portland, Oregon to **Belle** and her mate **Thonglaw**.

Britain's **Prince Philip** helps launch the newly organized World Wildlife Fund's campaign in New York.

"HEY I AIN'T MOVIN' THIS BUS 'TILL YOUSE MOVE TO THE REAR!"

Manners maven **Amy Vanderbilt** drafts a *"canon of courtesy"* for New York City bus drivers and recommends that they address men as *"Sir"* instead of *"Mac"* and *"Ma'am"* or *"Miss"* instead of *"Lady."*

SOON COMING TO YOUR NEGHBORHOOD

Mississippi, New York, Rhode Island, Virginia and Wisconsin now have laws requiring seat belts to be standard equipment in all new cars with New York's front seat belt law going into effect with 1965 models.

═══ WAY TO GO LIZZIE ═══

While dairy farmers receive lower prices, Americans break records in their consumption of milk and dairy products. Cows are producing an all-time high of 58,800,000,000 quarts of milk to serve the average person who drinks 145 quarts of milk and cream.

The Federal Government steps in to help dairy farmers by increasing the use of milk, butter and cheese in its School Lunch and School Milk programs.

HE LEARNED HIS PEAS AND CUCUMBERS

At the annual convention of the Future Farmers of America, **Warner A. Ross** of Toone, Tennessee is named the 1962 Star Farmer of America.

WHAT A YEAR IT WAS!

Popular Words & Expressions

1962

APOLLO
The spacecraft that will take American astronauts to the moon.

FELINOPHILE
A feline fan.

Ombudsman
An official intermediary who handles charges against the government.

beacher
A person who spends time at the beach.

FLIGHT RECORDER
Equipment in an airplane that records various facts such as velocity and altitude.

North

BLOCKBUSTING
When the threat of having less desirable people in the neighborhood convinces property owners to sell, often at reduced prices. The buyers then resell at higher prices.

KEY CLUB
A members-only exclusive nightclub.

RIDE-OUT
Blacks who emigrate from the south to the north, often with segregationist money.

CRYOBIOLOGY
A branch of science that concentrates on how freezing temperatures effect plants and animals.

LEM
Lunar excursion module, the section of the Apollo that will land on the moon.

SEND UP
To satirize.

bossa nova
A type of music from Brazil which incorporates jazz and samba rhythms. Also a dance.

SWINGING
A happy and hip person.

SPORTICIAN
A journalist who covers sports topics and events.

"Thermos"
cannot be owned by American Thermos, despite efforts to retain sole ownership of the word, and can officially be used by competitors and thermos lovers alike.

VOICEPRINT
A unique audio image of a person's voice.

WHAT A YEAR IT WAS!

63

Steadiness is built in! New shape gives you a firmer grip for sharp, clear pictures. Flash is built in, too. Complete **BROWNIE Super 27 Outfit** . . . less than $22.

Kodak gifts say: "Open me first" ...and save your Christmas in pictures!

Compact camera with built-in flash! No focusing indoors or out. With film, flashbulbs, batteries in **BROWNIE STARMITE Outfit** . . . less than $14.

Built-in exposure meter tells proper setting. No focusing, f/8 lens. Complete with everything you need! **BROWNIE STARMETER Outfit** . . . less than $29.

Electric eye sets lens opening automatically for beautiful movies. Light bar, lamps included in **KODAK Automatic 8 Movie Kit** . . . less than $63. Camera alone . . . less than $55.

Slides without guesswork! Automatic exposure setting, pop-up flash. **KODAK Automatic 35F Camera** . . . less than $100.

No trays! Smooth push-pull changing, budget price. **KODAK READYMATIC 500 Projector** . . . less than $70.

Make one setting for bright, clear movies with the **KODAK 8 Movie Camera** . . . less than $35. *Project films 4 ft. wide.* No threading—**BROWNIE 8 Movie Projector, A15** . . . less than $55.

Always welcome! KODAK Film for snaps, slides, movies. You can *depend* on the name Kodak!

Prices are subject to change without notice.

Kodak
TRADEMARK

EASTMAN KODAK COMPANY, Rochester 4, N.Y.
ENJOY WALT DISNEY'S "WONDERFUL WORLD OF COLOR" SUNDAY EVENINGS, NBC-TV

ENTERTAINMENT 1962

MOVIES

THE STUDIO EXECUTIVE BARGES IN

Racking up $35 million in production costs making it the most expensive picture of all time, 20th Century Fox studio head **Darryl F. Zanuck** flies to Paris to fire **CLEOPATRA** writer-director **Joseph Mankiewicz**.

Other SUPERBUDGET Spectaculars

How The West Was Won

The Longest Day

Barabbas

Lawrence Of Arabia

DANCE

Under the auspices of the State Department cultural exchange program, New York City Ballet is the first American ballet company to dance in the Bolshoi Theatre in Moscow.

WHAT A YEAR IT WAS!

TELEVISION

Johnny Carson takes over **Jack Paar's** slot as regular host of NBC's **The Tonight Show** and for the first time we hear: "Heeeeeeere's Johnny!"

MUSIC

Chubby Checker sets a record with the hit, *"The Twist"* which reaches the #1 position for the second time in two years.

WANNA' GO SEE A FLIK?

CAPE FEAR
The Chapman Report
The Children's Hour
Creation Of The Humanoids
david and lisa
The Day Mars Invaded Earth
Days Of Wine And Roses
Divorce-Italian Style
Dr. No
Five Finger Exercise
THE FOUR HORSEMEN OF THE APOCALYPSE
FREUD
Geronimo
Gigot
Gypsy
THE HAPPY THIEVES
HATARI!
I Like Mike
The Interns
Invasion Of The Star Creatures
JUMBO
KID GALAHAD
Lawrence Of Arabia

A VERY PRIVATE AFFAIR
ADVISE AND CONSENT
ALL FALL DOWN
BARABBAS
Billy Budd
Birdman Of Alcatraz
Boccaccio '70
Bon Voyage!
Boys' Night Out
The Brain That Wouldn't Die
The Cabinet Of Caligari

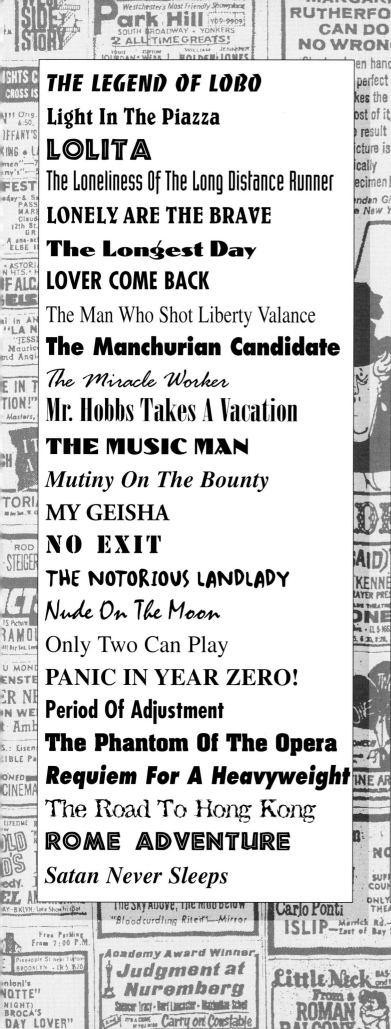

THE LEGEND OF LOBO

Light In The Piazza

LOLITA

The Loneliness Of The Long Distance Runner

LONELY ARE THE BRAVE

The Longest Day

LOVER COME BACK

The Man Who Shot Liberty Valance

The Manchurian Candidate

The Miracle Worker

Mr. Hobbs Takes A Vacation

THE MUSIC MAN

Mutiny On The Bounty

MY GEISHA

NO EXIT

THE NOTORIOUS LANDLADY

Nude On The Moon

Only Two Can Play

PANIC IN YEAR ZERO!

Period Of Adjustment

The Phantom Of The Opera

Requiem For A Heavyweight

The Road To Hong Kong

ROME ADVENTURE

Satan Never Sleeps

SERGEANTS 3

THE SLIME PEOPLE

SMOG

The Spiral Road

Strangers In The City

Sweet Bird Of Youth

Tender Is The Night

That Touch Of Mink

THIS IS NOT A TEST

To Kill A Mockingbird

Two For The Seesaw

Two Weeks In Another Town

The Underwater City

The Valiant

Walk On The Wild Side

Waltz Of The Toreadors

What Ever Happened To Baby Jane?

THE WEIRD ONES

YOJIMBO

1962
The Oscars

THE ACADEMY OF MOTION PICTUR[E]

The Santa Monica Civic Auditorium is the scene of the Oscar awards.

ROCK HUDSON *reads the winner for Best Supporting Actress.*

RITA MORENO *accepts the award and turns to the star-studded audience shouting: "I can't believe it!"*

JOAN CRAWFORD makes the presentation for Best Actor to MAXIMILIAN SCHELL.

WHAT A YEAR IT WAS!

BURT LANCASTER *announces the Best Actress winner. It is* SOPHIA LOREN, *the first actress in a foreign language film to be so honored.*

Beautiful GREER GARSON *accepts the Oscar on behalf of the absent Sophia.*

Then the moment the audience has been waiting for as FRED ASTAIRE *names the Best Picture of the year. The film is "WEST SIDE STORY" a musical tale of passions and conflict in New York slums.*

Co-director and producer ROBERT WISE *receives the statuette for his fellow artists.*

69

1962

The Academy Awards

"And The Winner Is..."

Citing the nasties that go on between actors competing for an Academy Award, **George C. Scott** declines an Oscar nomination for his supporting role as a pool-hall gambler in **The Hustler**.

Oscars Presented in 1962

BEST PICTURE
West Side Story

BEST ACTOR
Maximilian Schell, *Judgment At Nuremberg*

BEST ACTRESS
Sophia Loren, *Two Women*

BEST DIRECTOR
Robert Wise, Jerome Robbins, *West Side Story*

BEST SUPPORTING ACTOR
George Chakiris, *West Side Story*

BEST SUPPORTING ACTRESS
Rita Moreno, *West Side Story*

BEST SONG
"Moon River," *Breakfast At Tiffany's*

1962 Favorites (Oscars Presented In 1963)

BEST PICTURE
Lawrence Of Arabia

BEST ACTOR
Gregory Peck, *To Kill A Mockingbird*

BEST ACTRESS
Anne Bancroft, *The Miracle Worker*

BEST DIRECTOR
David Lean, *Lawrence Of Arabia*

BEST SUPPORTING ACTOR
Ed Begley, *Sweet Bird Of Youth*

BEST SUPPORTING ACTRESS
Patty Duke, *The Miracle Worker*

BEST SONG
"Days Of Wine And Roses," *Days Of Wine And Roses*

Peter O'Toole
Lawrence of Arabia

WHAT A YEAR IT WAS!

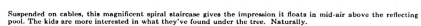

Happy Birthday

From *HIAWATHA* to *SPARTACUS*, **Universal has done much to revolutionize the entertainment world. It now looks forward to a second half-century of progress.**

Lana Turner is one of the stars participating in the celebration as Universal Pictures marks its 50th birthday.

The movie that sunk the submarine service in laughs, *OPERATION PETTICOAT* conditioned **Cary Grant** for his new role in *THAT TOUCH OF MINK*.

COME SEPTEMBER or any other month, **Sandra Dee** and **Bobby Darin** are top favorites.

Rock Hudson is a favorite in any language and at a recent German festival was honored as their outstanding box office favorite.

WHAT A YEAR IT WAS!

UNIVERSAL Pictures

Universal's galaxy of stars include **Tony Curtis** and **Janet Leigh**.

London bobbies hold back the crowd as **Kirk Douglas** arrives with his wife for a royal performance of SPARTACUS—England's way of honoring Universal's special occasion.

At the first overseas performance of this sweeping epic, **Princess Margaret** is on hand to congratulate everyone involved with the picture, including Mr. Douglas.

Universal President **Milton Rackmil** and **Cary Grant** cut the anniversary cake. The world's oldest motion picture company prepares for a second half-century of entertaining the wide, wide world.

MGM forks out $16,000 for a two-page advertisement in **The New York Times** *plugging its new film,* LOLITA.

SOMETHING'S GOT TO GIVE
WITH
SOMETHING'S GOT TO GIVE

Dean Martin bows out of SOMETHING'S GOT TO GIVE after his leading lady **Marilyn Monroe** is dropped from the movie.

Marilyn sheds 15 pounds before she begins filming SOMETHING'S GOT TO GIVE.

Marilyn is fired by 20th Century Fox and sued for damages after she misses 20 out of 32 work days during the filming of SOMETHING'S GOT TO GIVE.

Hedda Hopper predicts that **Marilyn** is at the end of her road after being fired from SOMETHING'S GOT TO GIVE.

Sophia Loren sues Bronston Productions for putting her name below **Charlton Heston's** on a Broadway billboard advertising *EL CID*.

Audrey Hepburn and **Shirley MacLaine** star in the film version of **Lillian Hellman's** *THE CHILDREN'S HOUR*, a controversial story about a lesbian relationship.

Hollywood queens **Joan Crawford** and **Bette Davis** begin filming *WHAT EVER HAPPENED TO BABY JANE?*, the story of two fading film stars who don't get along very well.

The manager of the Palace Theatre in Cambrai, France is fined 200 new francs for displaying an overly revealing poster of sex kitten **Brigitte Bardot**.

A nervous Actors Studio graduate, actress **Shelley Winters** gets a standing ovation after her lecture on "The Actor and the Modern Theatre" to 150 Harvard students.

WHO YOU CALLING A DUMMY?

Film star **Mary Pickford** presides over the opening of Hollywood's THE MOVIELAND WAX MUSEUM in Buena Park, California which features a life-size tableaux of **Clark Gable**, **Vivien Leigh** as well as **Charlie Chaplin**, **Wallace Beery**, **Will Rogers** and **Marie Dressler**.

WELL AIN'T THIS THE CAT'S MEOW

39-year-old **Ava Gardner** is set to play the female lead in *The Pink Panther* but excessive demands get her fired and replaced by French actress **Capucine**.

SHE'S GOT SOME GYPSY IN HER SOUL

Former First Lady **Mamie Eisenhower** has a good time on the set of *Gypsy* where she visits with old friend **Rosalind Russell**.

MASSIVE FALL-OUT

JAYNE MANSFIELD

loses the top of her dress as she dances The Twist in a Roman night spot.

Tippi Hedren, Alfred Hitchcock's new classic beauty discovery, stars in his new thriller, **THE BIRDS**, about which Mr. Hitchcock comments that his 700 trained bird actors work for birdseed.

WHAT A YEAR IT WAS!

BRINGING IN BIG BUCKS AT THE BOX OFFICE

Doris Day
Sandra Dee
Cary Grant
Rock Hudson
Burt Lancaster
Jerry Lewis
Elvis Presley
Frank Sinatra
Elizabeth Taylor
John Wayne

BOX OFFICE STARS OF TOMORROW

Ann-Margret
Richard Beymer
Michael Callan
Capucine
Bobby Darin
Peter Falk
James MacArthur
Yvette Mimieux
George Peppard
Suzanne Pleshette

Racing car buff Steve McQueen promises to give up racing until he's completed filming his current movie but says that he doesn't know if he's an actor dabbling in racing or vice versa.

Three days after **Darryl F. Zanuck's** arrival in New York, he is made president of 20th Century Fox.

- - - -

ON THE CHOPPING BLOCK

New 20th Century Fox head **Darryl Zanuck** trims the payroll of some high-priced executives and cancels three pictures scheduled for production including "Promise at Dawn" with **Ingrid Bergman**, "Take Her, She's Mine" starring **Jimmy Stewart** and James Joyce's "Ulysses" starring **Peter Sellers**.

- - - -

Following hours of turbulent meetings at Fox's New York headquarters, a brief announcement is made that 69-year-old **Spyros Skouras** is retiring for "reasons of health."

- - - -

In a civil antitrust action, the U.S. Justice Department forces MCA to divest itself of its talent agency.

After a long search Warner Bros. finally casts the originator of the role on Broadway, **Rex Harrison**, as Professor Higgins with **Audrey Hepburn** slated to play Eliza Doolittle in the film version of *My Fair Lady*, for which Warner pays a record $5.5 million for the movie rights.

BUT WILL HE WANT HIS OWN PRIVATE DRESSING CASTLE?

79-year-old **King Gustav VI Adolph** of Sweden takes a walk-on part in the film version of the Swedish fairy tale *The Wonderful Adventures of Nils.*

A HANDS-ON EXPERIENCE

700 adoring fans watch as Sophia Loren gets her palm prints immortalized in cement at Grauman's Chinese Theatre.

1962

Actor **DICK POWELL** is convalescing at his home in Hollywood after undergoing radiation treatments for cancer in his neck and chest.

LANA TURNER is hospitalized after collapsing at a movie-set celebration for her birthday.

Dick Powell

Following separation from her third husband, **TONY CURTIS**, film actress **JANET LEIGH** is found unconscious in a Manhattan hotel room bathroom.

SAL MINEO is fined $50 and has his license revoked after three convictions for speeding.

HAPPY BIRTHDAY SAMMY
Samuel Goldwyn celebrates his 80th birthday and 50 years in the motion picture business.

FAMOUS BIRTHS

Ally Sheedy
Andrew McCarthy
Cary Elwes
Demi Moore
Emilio Estevez
Jennifer Jason Leigh
Jim Carrey
Joan Cusack
Jodie Foster
Lou Diamond Phillips
Ralph Fiennes
Tom Cruise
Wesley Snipes

PASSING
Director of such classic films as *"The Jazz Singer," "White Christmas"* and *"Casablanca,"* for which he won an Academy Award, **MICHAEL CURTIZ** dies at age 73.

ANOTHER HIT FOR CARY!

That Touch of Mink starring **CARY GRANT** breaks box office records at Radio City Music Hall surpassing *North by Northwest* which also starred Mr. Grant.

SPLENDOR IN THE INTERNATIONAL GRASSES

Recently divorced Hollywood star **NATALIE WOOD** tours Europe with **WARREN BEATTY** where they attend the Cannes Film Festival.

WHAT A YEAR IT WAS!

TELEVISION 1962

What's Playing On TV This Week

The Adventures Of Ozzie & Harriet

The Andy Griffith Show

The Andy Williams Show

Bachelor Father

Beany And Cecil

Ben Casey

The Bob Newhart Show

Bonanza

The Bugs Bunny Show

The Bullwinkle Show

Candid Camera

Car 54, Where Are You?

Cheyenne

The Danny Thomas Show

Death Valley Days

The Defenders

Dennis The Menace

The Detectives

The Dick Powell Show

The Dick Van Dyke Show

The Dinah Shore Chevy Show

The Donna Reed Show

Dr. Kildare

The Ed Sullivan Show

Ensign O'Toole

Father Knows Best

Father Of The Bride

The Flintstones

The Garry Moore Show

The Gertrude Berg Show

Gunsmoke

Have Gun Will Travel

Hawaiian Eye

Hazel

I've Got A Secret

It's A Man's World

The Jack Benny Show

The Joey Bishop Show

Laramie

Lassie

The Lawrence Welk Show

Leave It To Beaver

The Many Loves Of Dobie Gillis

The Match Game

Maverick

Meet The Press

The Merv Griffin Show

Mister Ed

My Three Sons

Password

The Perry Como Show

Perry Mason

The Price Is Right

Rawhide

The Real McCoys

The Red Skelton Show

The Rifleman

Route 66

77 Sunset Strip

Tell It To Groucho

To Tell The Truth

The Twilight Zone

The Untouchables

What's My Line?

What's New On The TV Block

The Alfred Hitchcock Hour

Combat!

Davey And Goliath

The Eleventh Hour

The Gallant Men

Going My Way

I'm Dickens—He's Fenster

The Jack Paar Program

Jackie Gleason And His
  American Scene Magazine

The Lloyd Bridges Show

The Lucy Show

McHale's Navy

Mr. Smith Goes To Washington

The New Loretta Young Show

The Tonight Show
  Starring Johnny Carson

The Virginian

The Wide Country

Alfred Hitchcock

Faces On The Boob Tube

Don Adams
Jack Albertson
Don Ameche
Morey Amsterdam
Eddie "Rochester"
  Anderson
Fred Astaire
Jim Backus
Kaye Ballard
Frances Bavier
Ralph Bellamy
Ted Bessell
Barbara Billingsley
Bill Bixby
Richard Boone
Shirley Booth
Ernest Borgnine
Walter Brennan
Beau Bridges
James Broderick
Raymond Burr
Carol Burnett
Edd "Kookie" Byrnes
Sebastian Cabot
Judy Carne
Leo G. Carroll
Pat Carroll
Angela Cartwright
Richard Chamberlain
Lee J. Cobb
Chuck Connors
Bob Conrad
Tim Conway
Jackie Cooper
Richard Crenna
Vic Damone
Don DeFore
William Demarest
Bob Denver
John Derek
Bruce Dern
Troy Donohue
Clint Eastwood
Buddy Ebsen
Shelley Fabares
Norman Fell
Joe Flynn
John Forsythe
James Franciscus
Gale Gordon

Lorne Greene
Shecky Greene
Fred Gwynne
Buddy Hackett
Pat Harrington, Jr.
Florence Henderson
Earl Holliman
Ronny Howard
Marty Ingalls
Arte Johnson
Stubby Kaye
Boris Karloff
Gene Kelly
Don Knotts
Michael Landon
Mary Livingstone
June Lockhart
Allen Ludden
Paul Lynde
Gavin MacLeod
Fred MacMurray
Rose Marie
E.G. Marshall
Jerry Mathers
Ed McMahon
Martin Milner
Candy Moore
Garry Moore
Mary Tyler Moore
Vic Morrow
Leslie Nielsen
Jay North
Ryan O'Neal
Fess Parker
Robert Reed
Carl Reiner
Burt Reynolds
Gena Rowlands
Nipsey Russell
Irene Ryan
Rod Serling
Robert Stack
Marlo Thomas
Leslie Uggams
Dennis Weaver
Adam West
Betty White
Jane Wyatt
Dick York
Robert Young

TOP RATED TELEVISION PROGRAMS

WINTER

The Bob Hope Christmas Show
Wagon Train
Bonanza
The Garry Moore Show
Disney's World Of Color
Dr. Kildare
Rawhide
Perry Mason
Hazel
The Red Skelton Show

TOP RATED TELEVISION PROGRAMS

SUMMER

Miss America Pageant
The Lucy-Desi Comedy Hour
The Ed Sullivan Show
Dr. Kildare
Wagon Train
Bonanza
Perry Mason
Ben Casey
Saturday Night At The Movies
The Defenders

In one of the fastest climbs in television history, **THE BEVERLY HILLBILLIES** takes the top spot in the Nielsen ratings after only five weeks.

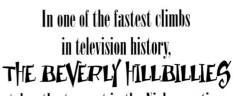

Bluegrass stars Lester Flatt and Earl Scruggs write and record the theme song THE BALLAD OF JED CLAMPETT for the new television program, **THE BEVERLY HILLBILLIES.**

THE JETSONS, the first program to be carried by ABC in color, premieres.

THAT LITTLE 'OL PIE-THROWER HITS THE BIG TIME

With a penchant for pie-in-the-face humor, Detroit local **Soupy Sales** is picked up by ABC for a prime time spot.

INTO THE FRYING PAN

Julia Child kicks off her PBS cooking show, *The French Chef.*

1962

THE SHOTS SEEN AROUND THE WORLD

The Statue of Liberty, President Kennedy's news conference, a portion of a baseball game, pictures of buffalo and an Indian chief in South Dakota are the first images transmitted to Europe using the new Telstar system. Europe responds and sends America shots of Big Ben in London, the Sistine Chapel and fisherman in Italy and reindeer in Sweden.

TOP RATED AMERICAN TELEVISION PROGRAMS ABROAD

JAPAN:

Rawhide (Westerns are the most popular)
Ben Casey
Dennis The Menace
I Love Lucy
The Untouchables
Father Knows Best

SCOTLAND:

Ben Casey

WALES:

Bonanza

ITALY:

Perry Mason

WEST GERMANY:

77 Sunset Strip
Perry Mason

MEXICO:

Gunsmoke
Mike Hammer

AND NOW A VERY, VERY LOUD WORD FROM OUR SPONSOR

A manufacturer of sound-testing equipment releases a study revealing that 65% of commercials on television are aired at significantly higher sound levels than the regular programs and these are some of the culprits:

COMMERCIAL	% LOUDER	PROGRAM
Joy Detergent	78%	The Rebel
Zest Soap	59%	Law Of The Plainsman
Ivory Soap	59%	Danger Man
Anacin	59%	Highway Patrol
Lifebuoy	41%	77 Sunset Strip
Dial Soap	41%	Surfside Six

Conversely, **Goodrich Tire**, **Kraft** and **Lestoil** run their commercials at lower decibels.

The only roof as pretty as this one...

is no roof at all

It's mighty hard to improve on a classic. And that's what Comet's roof has become. The '63 edition is shown above: jaunty, elegant. The only direction to go was off! Result: two Comet convertibles, one an S-22 with bucket seats. So if you prefer the sun, moon, and stars for a roof, choose a Comet top-downer. Prefer a classic? Pick the sedan. Either way you'll flip <u>your</u> lid.

'63 MERCURY COMET

COMET · METEOR · MONTEREY: PRODUCTS OF *Ford* MOTOR COMPANY · LINCOLN-MERCURY DIVISION

1962

The United States now has 67 educational television stations throughout the country.

PUTTING THEIR FEET TO THE FIRE

The FCC holds a series of hearings on network programming examining the polices of CBS, NBC and ABC.

BEWARE OF THE VAST WASTELAND

FCC Chairman Newton Minow warns that television must be expanded to UHF or *"soon we will have unnecessarily few people deciding what larger and larger numbers of people will be seeing."*

FIGHTING BACK

In order to stimulate educational programming, Congress authorizes $32 million to be used for that purpose.

Congress passes legislation requiring that all television sets shipped interstate be equipped to receive UHF and VHF signals.

SERIES

Humor	*THE BOB NEWHART SHOW*
Drama	*THE DEFENDERS*
Variety	*THE GARRY MOORE SHOW*
News	*HUNTLEY-BRINKLEY REPORT*

ENTERTAINERS

Actor	**E.G. MARSHALL** *The Defenders*
Actress	**SHIRLEY BOOTH** *Hazel*
Performer (Variety or Musical)	**CAROL BURNETT** *The Garry Moore Show*
Comedy Writer	**CARL REINER** *The Dick Van Dyke Show*

– PASSING –

Television comedian and cigar aficionado **ERNIE KOVACS** dies at age 42.

FAMOUS BIRTHS

Aida Turturro	Jon Stewart
Anthony Edwards	Kristy McNichol
Brandon Cruz	Laura San Giacomo
Dylan McDermott	Melissa Sue Anderson
Eddie Izzard	Rob Morrow
Eriq La Salle	Rosie O'Donnell
Jeremy Gelbwaks	

CBS Evening News gets an anchorman, commentator **Walter Cronkite.**

HE CAN PUT HIS STETHOSCOPE AROUND MY NECK ANYTIME

Freshman student nurses at New York's St. Vincent's Hospital are given permission to stay up past their 10:30 curfew to watch *BEN CASEY* on Monday nights.

THE TIME OF HIS LIFE

Playwright and novelist **William Saroyan** is added to the list of first-rate writers writing for television.

29-year-old **Carol Burnett**, one of the funniest faces on television, does a TV special with **Julie Andrews** called *JULIE AND CAROL AT CARNEGIE HALL.*

THE VIRGINIAN is the first 90-minute series.

THE FLOOD, a musical dance drama written for TV by **Igor Stravinsky**, premieres on CBS.

Covering the United Nations for ABC, **Mal Goode** becomes the first black network correspondent.

New York's Statler Hilton hotel introduces a half-hour in-room cable TV tour of the city, featuring tips on restaurants, sightseeing and special events.

Over 60 million television viewers watch as Astronaut **John H. Glenn** is launched into space while a total of 135 million people tune in some time during the day.

DON'T MESS WITH THE DUKE

WNBC-TV scraps the airing of *Biography of the Duke* after the Duke of Windsor threatens the network with a lawsuit charging invasion of privacy.

Lucille Ball becomes

president of *Desilu* Studios after she buys out ex-husband **Desi Arnaz** for over $2 million.

WHAT A YEAR IT WAS!

83

1962

THE NOT SO GOLDEN DAYS OF RADIO

In a speech before the National Association of Broadcasters, **Newton Minow** voices his concern over the uncertain economic health of the radio industry as one-third of the nation's radio stations report a loss.

THEY'RE STILL TUNING IN

183,800,000 radio sets are currently being used in American homes.

New York's **WOR** celebrates its 40th year on the air, with its successful 24 hours a day programming including over 20 hours of talk.

Accepting the George Foster Peabody Award, FCC chairman **Newton Minow** calls radio a "casbah of pitchmen."

The FCC orders a freeze on permits to construct new radio stations.

Amateur radio operators celebrate the 50th year of licensed radio operation.

With the help of **Edward R. Murrow**, CBS radio personality **John Henry Faulk** is awarded $2.8 million in a libel suit against a sponsor who accused him of being a Communist.

THE SUSPENSE IS FINALLY OVER

On the radio since 1942, the very popular program **SUSPENSE** stops airing as does **YOURS TRULY, JOHNNY DOLLAR**, which began broadcasting in 1949.

The POPULAR SONGS

POPULAR MUSIC

Baby, It's You	*The Shirelles*
Big Girls Don't Cry	*Frankie Valli & The 4 Seasons*
Blowin' In The Wind	*Bob Dylan*
Break It To Me Gently	*Brenda Lee*
Breaking Up Is Hard To Do	*Neil Sedaka*
Can't Help Falling In Love	*Elvis Presley*
Cotton Fields	*The Highwaymen*
Crying In The Rain	*The Everly Brothers*
Devil Woman	*Marty Robbins*
Do You Love Me	*The Contours*
Don't Break The Heart That Loves You	*Connie Francis*
Don't Hang Up	*The Orlons*
Dream Baby	*Roy Orbison*
Duke Of Earl	*Gene Chandler*
Go Away Little Girl	*Steve Lawrence*
Good Luck Charm	*Elvis Presley*
Havin' A Party	*Sam Cooke*
He's A Rebel	*The Crystals*
I Can't Stop Loving You	*Ray Charles*
It Keeps Right On A-Hurtin'	*Johnny Tillotson*
I've Been Everywhere	*Hank Snow*
Johnny Angel	*Shelly Fabares*
Johnny Get Angry	*Joanie Sommers*
Let Me In	*The Sensations*
Letter Full Of Tears	*Gladys Knight & The Pips*
Limbo Rock	*Chubby Checker*
The Loco-Motion	*Little Eva*
Love Letters	*Ketty Lester*
The Man Who Shot Liberty Valance	*Gene Pitney*
Mashed Potato Time	*Dee Dee Sharp*
Misery Loves Company	*Porter Wagoner*
Monster Mash	*Bobby "Boris" Pickett & The Crypt Kickers*
The One Who Really Loves You	*Mary Wells*
Only Love Can Break A Heart	*Gene Pitney*

Palisades Park	*Freddy Cannon*
Party Lights	*Claudine Clark*
Patches	*Dickey Lee*
Peppermint Twist	*Joey Dee & The Starliters*
Ramblin' Rose	*Nat "King" Cole*
Return To Sender	*Elvis Presley*
Roses Are Red	*Bobby Vinton*
Sealed With A Kiss	*Brian Hyland*
She Cried	*Jay & The Americans*
She Thinks I Still Care	*George Jones*
She's Got You	*Patsy Cline*
Sheila	*Tommy Roe*
Sherry	*Frankie Valli & The 4 Seasons*
Shout! Shout! (Knock Yourself Out)	*Ernie Maresca*
Slow Twistin'	*Chubby Checker*
Soldier Boy	*The Shirelles*
The Stripper	*David Rose*
Stubborn Kind Of Fellow	*Marvin Gaye*
Surfin' Safari	*The Beach Boys*
Theme From Dr. Kildare	*Richard Chamberlain*
The Twist	*Chubby Checker*
Twist And Shout	*The Isley Brothers*
Twistin' The Night Away	*Sam Cooke*
Up On The Roof	*The Drifters*
The Wah Watusi	*The Orlons*
Walk On By	*Leroy Van Dyke*
The Wanderer	*Dion*
What's Your Name	*Don And Juan*
When I Fall In Love	*The Lettermen*
Wolverton Mountain	*Claude King*
You Don't Know Me	*Ray Charles*
Young World	*Rick Nelson*

1962

THE BEATLES
— THE BEGINNINGS —

Ringo Starr replaces **Pete Best** on drums.

WAY TO GO, DECCA
Citing that *"groups of guitars are on the way out,"* Decca Records rejects **The Beatles** after they audition for the label.

The Beatles audition for producer **George Martin** at EMI-Parlophone in London. He signs the group following their failed audition at Decca.

George Martin produces the single *Love Me Do* combined with *P.S. I Love You* at his first recording session with **The Beatles** and after 16 takes is satisfied.

The Beatles make their television debut, appearing on the BBC program "Teenager's Turn" to play **Roy Orbison's** *Dream Baby*.

Brian Epstein signs **The Beatles** to a management deal.

Peter Jones of the *LONDON DAILY MIRROR* interviews **The Beatles** and concludes they are *"a nothing group."*

Stuart Sutcliffe, an original member of **The Beatles**, dies of cerebral paralysis caused by a brain hemorrhage.

The Beatles are one of the opening acts for a **Little Richard** concert at New Brighton Towne, Liverpool.

NEW RECORDING ARTISTS

Herb Alpert &
The Tijuana Brass

The Beach Boys

Booker T. &
The MG's

Gene Chandler

Bob Dylan

The 4 Seasons

Marvin Gaye

Bobby Goldsboro

Jay &
The Americans

Jack Jones

Carole King

Willie Nelson

Peter, Paul & Mary

Tommy Roe

The Supremes

Bobby Vinton

Dionne Warwick

A record number of discs go "gold" this year, including five singles and 37 LP's.

WANNA BUY A RECORD?
IT'LL COST YOU:
$ 3.98   (mono album)
4.98   (stereo album)
.98   (45 rpm disc)

RETAIL SALES OF PHONOGRAPH RECORDS
A Record $550 Million
LP's: 75% of Total Sales
Stereo: 40% of Album Sales

WHAT A YEAR IT WAS!

1962 ADVERTISEMENT

To widen the audience for stereo records—COLUMBIA RECORD CLUB now offers this fine

STEREO PHONOGRAPH $7.95

at far below actual cost...only

$39.95 VALUE

if you begin your membership with any one of the stereo records shown below — and agree to buy a record every four weeks during the coming year

ONE YEAR WARRANTY AGAINST DEFECTS
Columbia Compact Stereo Phonographs come with one-year guarantee on service and parts.

HERE is a unique opportunity to enjoy, right in your own home, the newest dimension in recorded music — Stereophonic Sound! Yes, for only $7.95 (plus postage), you can own this new Columbia Compact Stereo Phonograph — a $39.95 value — that enables you to hear music reproduced in a way never before possible with ordinary phonographs.

We make this offer as a demonstration of the Columbia Record Club's remarkable Bonus Plan . . . a plan that enables you, as a member, to acquire this fine Stereo Phonograph at just a fraction of its value just by purchasing superb stereophonic records which you in any case would want to add to your record library.

HOW TO GET YOUR STEREO PHONOGRAPH. You begin your membership by selecting any one of the 12" stereo records shown here — at the list price. Indicate your choice on the coupon . . . and at the same time, be sure to indicate in which one of the Club's four musical Divisions you wish to enroll: Classical; Listening and Dancing; Broadway, Movies, Television and Musical Comedies; Jazz.

Then simply return the coupon — without money — and you will promptly receive the stereo record you have selected, together with a bill for $12.93 (that's $4.98 for the record, $7.95 for the phonograph), plus postage. (If you select a higher priced record, you will be billed accordingly.) Upon receipt of payment, we will ship your phonograph.

FREE STEREO MUSIC MAGAZINE . . . Every four weeks you will receive, free, the Club's entertaining and informative music Magazine — which will describe fifty or more stereo recordings from every field of music.

You may choose any of the selections described, no matter which musical Division you have joined . . . and the records you want will be mailed and billed to you at the list price of $4.98 (Classical $5.98; occasional Original Cast recordings somewhat higher), plus a small mailing and handling charge.

Your only membership obligation is to purchase a record every four weeks during the coming year . . . and you may discontinue membership at any time thereafter. If you decide to continue as a member after fulfilling your enrollment agreement, you need not purchase any specified number of records — but for every two selections you do accept, you will receive a stereo bonus record of your choice free.

MAIL COUPON NOW! The number of phonographs manufactured for this offer is limited — so act now!

BEGIN YOUR MEMBERSHIP WITH ANY ONE OF THESE STEREO RECORDS

HEAVENLY — Hello, Young Lovers; Stranger In Paradise; 10 more — JOHNNY MATHIS
6. Also: Moonlight Becomes You, That's All, etc. $4.98

ROGER WILLIAMS GREATEST HITS — Autumn Leaves; Near You; Tammy; 9 More — KAPP
25. Also: September Song, I Got Rhythm, etc. . . . $4.98

GUITAR'S GREATEST HITS — Guitar Boogie, Rebel-Rouser, Raunchy, Caravan — 8 More
104. Also: The Third Man Theme, Rumble, etc. $4.98

LERNER & LOEWE — Camelot — RICHARD BURTON, JULIE ANDREWS and Original Broadway Cast — COLUMBIA
143. "Most lavish and beautiful musical."—Kilgallen. . . $6.98

The Harmonicats — MOON RIVER; EL CID; LA DOLCE VITA; 9 More Movie Hits
33. Also: Around the World, Guns of Navarone, etc. . . . $4.98

TIME OUT — THE DAVE BRUBECK QUARTET — COLUMBIA
52. Take Five, Kathy's Waltz, Everybody's Jumpin', etc. . . $4.98

WEST SIDE STORY — Original Soundtrack Recording — COLUMBIA
147. "Most adventurous musical ever made."—Life. $5.98

Rhapsody in Blue / An American in Paris — Leonard Bernstein plays Gershwin — COLUMBIA
176. "Fierce impact, momentum."—N.Y. World-Tele. . .$5.98

HAWAII — The Fabulous 50th State — SAM MAKIA and the Makapuu Beach Boys
118. King Kamehameha, Blue Hawaii, 10 more. . . . $4.98

GREAT MOTION PICTURE THEMES — EXODUS; NEVER ON SUNDAY; THE APARTMENT; plus 13 more
115. Also: Some Like It Hot, The Magnificent Seven, etc. . $4.98

GRAND CANYON SUITE — PHILADELPHIA ORCH., ORMANDY — COLUMBIA
173. This brilliant musical painting is a must. $5.98

REX HARRISON, JULIE ANDREWS — MY FAIR LADY — ORIGINAL CAST RECORDING
145. The best-selling Original Cast recording. $5.98

THE PLATTERS Encore of Golden Hits — Twilight Time, My Prayer, Only You, 9 more
1. Also: The Great Pretender, Enchanted, etc. . .$4.98

THE BLUE DANUBE — A Johann Strauss Festival — COLUMBIA
178. ". . .a real specialist at Strauss."—High Fidel. $5.98

JOHNNY HORTON'S GREATEST HITS — Battle of New Orleans, Sink the Bismarck, North to Alaska — COLUMBIA
12. Also: Comanche, The Mansion You Stole, etc. . . $4.98

LORD'S PRAYER — MORMON TABERNACLE CHOIR — BATTLE HYMN OF THE REPUBLIC; THE LORD'S PRAYER 9 MORE
169. Also: Londonderry Air; Holy, Holy, Holy, etc. . . $5.98

RAY CONNIFF — Memories are Made of This; Tammy; My Foolish Heart; 10 more — COLUMBIA
225. Also: No Other Love, Love Me Tender, etc. $4.98

CHOPIN: The 14 Waltzes — Brailowsky — COLUMBIA
187. "Elegant. . .tone is crystalline."—N.Y. Times. . . .$5.98

THE WORLD'S GREATEST THEMES — FERRANTE & TEICHER — UNITED ARTISTS
47. Romance, Theme from "The Apartment," etc. $4.98

SING ALONG WITH MITCH — MITCH MILLER AND THE GANG — COLUMBIA
8. That Old Gang of Mine, Sweet Violets, etc. $4.98

COLUMBIA RECORD CLUB
165 West 46th Street, New York 36, N.Y.

★ Feather-light tone arm with two jeweled styli and sensitive stereo cartridge
★ Lock-cornered wood cabinet — covered with washable, pyroxylin treated fabric
★ 4-speed turret selector which enables you to play all 16, 33, 45 or 78 rpm records
★ Two powerful speaker units connected by 8-foot cords for maximum stereo effect
★ Plays BOTH stereophonic AND regular high-fidelity records
★ Two controls — volume and balance
★ UL approved — A.C. only
★ Portable — removable speaker units

SEND NO MONEY — Mail Coupon to receive your Stereo Phonograph for $7.95

COLUMBIA RECORD CLUB, Dept. 601-6
Stereophonic Phonograph Section
165 West 46th Street, New York 36, N. Y.

Please send me—at once—the stereo record I have indicated at the right. With my record I will receive a bill for $12.93 (that's $4.98 for the record, $7.95 for the phonograph), plus postage. (If I select a higher priced record, I will be billed accordingly.) Upon payment of this bill, I will receive a Columbia Compact Stereo Phonograph. Enroll me in the following Division of the Club:

(Check one box only)
☐ Classical   ☐ Listening & Dancing   ☐ Jazz
☐ Broadway, Movies, Television and Musical Comedies

My only obligation thereafter is to purchase a record every four weeks during the coming year at list price, plus small mailing and handling charge. I may discontinue membership at any time after purchasing these records. Should I continue my membership thereafter, I need not purchase any specified number of records — but for every two selections I accept, I will receive a stereo bonus record free.

Name. . . . .
(Please Print)
Address. . . . .
City. . . . . .Zone. . . . .State. . . . .
APO, FPO addressees: write for special offer
If you want this membership credited to an established Columbia or Epic record dealer, authorized to accept subscriptions, fill in the following:
Dealer's Name and Address. P60

CIRCLE ONE NUMBER BELOW
1. Platters Encore of Golden Hits ($4.98)
6. Heavenly — Johnny Mathis ($4.98)
8. Sing Along With Mitch Miller ($4.98)
12. Johnny Horton's Greatest Hits ($4.98)
25. Roger Williams Greatest Hits ($4.98)
33. Moon River — The Harmonicats ($4.98)
47. Great Themes—Ferrante/Teicher ($4.98)
52. Time Out — Dave Brubeck ($4.98)
104. Guitars Greatest Hits ($4.98)
115. Great Motion Picture Themes ($4.98)
119. Hawaii ($4.98)
143. Camelot ($6.98)
145. My Fair Lady ($5.98)
147. West Side Story ($4.98)
169. The Lord's Prayer ($5.98)
173. Grofe: Grand Canyon Suite ($5.98)
176. Gershwin: Rhapsody in Blue ($5.98)
178. Strauss: The Blue Danube ($5.98)
187. Chopin: The 14 Waltzes ($5.98)
225. Memories Are Made of This ($4.98)

TB

® "Columbia," ℗ @ "Epic," @ Marcas Reg. @ Columbia Records Distribution Corp., 1962

87

1962
All That Jazz

MOST POPULAR JAZZ ARTIST

Ray Charles

MOST SUCCESSFUL JAZZ INSTRUMENTALISTS

Dave Brubeck *Piano*
Stan Getz *Tenor Sax*
Miles Davis *Trumpet*
Pete Fountain *Clarinet*
Herbie Mann *Flute*

After 33 years of playing "Auld Lang Syne" at The Roosevelt Hotel's Grill Room, **Guy Lombardo** heads to Florida for a new gig.

Duke Ellington serves as honorary host of the First International Jazz Festival in the town where his father and uncle were once butlers at the White House.

Imported from Brazil, U.S. jazz gets a new musical style called *bossa nova*, which combines American jazz with the Brazilian samba. Saxophonists **Stan Getz**, **Zoot Sims**, **Bud Shank** and **Sonny Rollins** are among the musicians popularizing this sound.

An American jazz orchestra is heard for the first time in Russia when **Benny Goodman** goes on a six-week tour with a special band.

- - - - -

Greeting **Benny Goodman** at a reception at the American Embassy in Moscow, Soviet Premier **Nikita Khrushchev** congratulates The Swing King while at the same time declaring that he is not a jazz fan, doesn't dance and is just there to drink the beer.

12-YEAR-OLD STEVELAND MORRIS JUDKINS, RENAMED *Little Stevie Wonder*, RECORDS HIS FIRST SINGLE, "THANK YOU FOR LOVING ME ALL THE WAY," FOR MOTOWN RECORDS AND THOUGH THE RECORD IS NOT A SUCCESS, HE IS BILLED AS THE 12-YEAR-OLD GENIUS.

Motown Records launches a two-month tour of the U.S. kicking off in Washington D.C. with **The Miracles**, **Mary Wells**, **The Supremes**, **Marvin Gaye** *and* **Little Stevie Wonder**.

MOTOWN RECORDS releases the first production by *The Miracles*, "You've Really Got A Hold On Me," written by lead singer-songwriter, **Smokey Robinson**.

Aretha Franklín auditions at Columbia with *"My Funny Valentine"* and SAM COOKE'S *"Navajo Trail"* and is signed to a contract the next day.

FAMOUS BIRTHS

Anthony Kiedis
Clint Black
Flea
Garth Brooks
Jon Bon Jovi
Paula Abdul
Sheryl Crow
Tommy Lee

WHAT A YEAR IT WAS!

He's Doing It His Way

Recording for his own record label, Reprise, for the past two years, **Frank Sinatra** records his final session for Capitol Records in Hollywood with *"I Gotta Right to Sing the Blues."*

Tony Bennett makes his first appearance at Carnegie Hall.

Sinatra

33-year-old crooner **Eddie Fisher** opens at Hollywood's Cocoanut Grove.

Bennett

Thank Heaven For Big Boys

Over 4,000 fans flock to Griffith Park in Los Angeles to hear 73-year-old French troubadour **Maurice Chevalier** perform with his familiar straw hat tipped to one side.

WOMEN ON THE AIRWAVES

Patsy Cline	**Sue Thompson**
Little Eva	**Mary Wells**
Shelley Fabares	**The Marvelettes**
Connie Francis	**The Orlons**
Brenda Lee	**The Shirelles**
Timo Yuro	

Billboard magazine drops the *"Western"* from its chart title and substitutes *"Hot Country Singles."*

ALAN FREED appears at his payola trial in New York testifying that he received $2,000 in 1958 from Cognat Distributors for a promise to play their records on his New York radio show. He also worked a similar deal with Superior Records for $700. He pleads guilty, is fined $300 and given six months probation.

WHAT A YEAR IT WAS!

RICKY NELSON signs a 20-year contract with Decca Records.

•

ELVIS PRESLEY receives his 29th gold record for *"Can't Help Falling In Love."*

•

THEY LOVE TO SING IN A MER I CA

British group **The Tornadoes** record the instrumental *"Telstar"* which becomes the first British rock song to hit No. 1 on the charts in America.

A new group called

THE ROLLING STONES, featuring **MICK JAGGER, KEITH RICHARDS** and **BRIAN JONES**, make their performing debut at the Marquee Club in London.

Bob Dylan makes his first appearance at Carnegie Hall.

Columbia releases *"Bob Dylan."*

1962

THE FOLK SCENE

The first protest song to hit the Top 40 is **The Kingston Trio's** recording of *"Where Have All The Flowers Gone?"*

Folk singer **Pete Seeger's** 1955 contempt conviction for refusing to answer questions before the House Un-American Activities Committee is reversed by the U.S. Court of Appeals.

FACES ON THE FOLK SCENE

Peter, Paul and Mary	**Carolyn Hester**
New Christy Minstrels	**Judy Collins**
Joan Baez	**Bonnie Dobson**

Warner Bros. Records signs the folk trio **Peter, Paul and Mary** who record *"If I Had A Hammer."*

The Springfields, a British folk trio that includes **Dusty** and brother **Tom Springfield**, has a top twenty hit in the U.S. with *"Silver Threads And Golden Needles."*

21-year-old **Joan Baez** sells more records than any other female folk singer in history and in a single week has two albums at the top of the charts.

GRAMMY awards

Song Of The Year	***What Kind Of Fool Am I*** Leslie Bricusse & Anthony Newley, songwriters
Record Of The Year	***I Left My Heart In San Francisco*** Tony Bennett
Album Of The Year	***The First Family*** Vaughn Meader
Best Solo Vocal Performance, Male	***I Left My Heart In San Francisco*** Tony Bennett
Best Solo Vocal Performance, Female	***Ella Swings Brightly With Nelson Riddle*** Ella Fitzgerald
Best Country & Western Performance	***Funny Way Of Laughin'*** Burl Ives
Best Rock & Roll Recording	***Alley Cat*** Bent Fabric
Best Rhythm & Blues Recording	***I Can't Stop Loving You*** Ray Charles
Best Folk Recording	***If I Had A Hammer*** Peter, Paul and Mary
Best New Artist	Robert Goulet

WHAT A YEAR IT WAS!

How do you keep roll-l-l-ing?

You give yourself this *quick, fresh lift!*

Where do you get that little extra oomph you need to carry you through? Right here—from 7-Up! Seven-Up brings you brand new energy in only two to six minutes! And that isn't all. You get a brand new taste in your mouth, too. And a fine, frisky, fresh-as-spring feeling all over. Could you use that now? C'mon. It's *always* 7-Up time!

FOR FRESH TASTE, THIRST QUENCHING, QUICK LIFT . . . "FRESH UP" WITH SEVEN-UP!

91

Pulitzer Prize for Music
The Crucible
ROBERT WARD

Classical CHATTER

THE NEW YORK TIMES refers to composer John Cage's New York premiere of *Music Walk With Dancer* as "Mayhem."

Stravinsky's new 15-minute cantata *A Sermon, A Narrative And A Prayer* is considered an impressive achievement.

800 limousines line the streets as patrons of the arts, with **Jackie Kennedy** as special guest of honor, show up for a performance at Philharmonic Hall, the first completed building of the Lincoln Center for the Performing Arts. Featuring **Leonard Bernstein** and the New York Philharmonic, other performers include tenors **Richard Tucker** and **Jon Vickers** and soprano **Eileen Farrell**.

Eugene Ormandy's Philadelphia Orchestra is the first symphonic group to sell one million LP's in a single year with **Leonard Bernstein's New York Philharmonic** not far behind that number.

The **New York Philharmonic** moves to Lincoln Center after giving its last concert at Carnegie Hall, its 6,456th since 1891.

Leopold Stokowski celebrates his 80th birthday by conducting the newly-formed **American Symphony Orchestra**, comprised of young musicians, which receives cheers at its Carnegie Hall debut. He is also guest conductor of the **Philadelphia Orchestra**, commemorating 50 years of association with that orchestra.

The Edinburgh Festival is offering 25 of Soviet composer **Dmitry Shostakovich's** works in three weeks, including six of the symphonies, eight quartets and two concertos.

Conducting a 96-piece orchestra in San Francisco, **Boston Pops** conductor **Arthur Fiedler** does a three-minute baroque version of **Chubby Checker's** *The Twist*.

Erich Leinsdorf named successor to **Charles Munch** as conductor of the **Boston Symphony**.

After the chorus in West Berlin's **Deutsche Oper** chanted the final line of **Benjamin Britten's** new *War Requiem*, a protest against the destruction caused by World War II, the stunned audience sits in silence which is then followed by thunderous applause.

Picking up his baton in San Francisco for his first public concert in America in over thirty years, 85-year-old cellist **Pablo Casals** begins a two-year worldwide personal crusade for peace.

Paris' matriarch of music, 75-year-old **Nadia Boulanger**, becomes the first woman to conduct an entire concert of the New York Philharmonic.

For the first time in 52 years, 80-year-old composer **Igor Stravinsky** visits his native Russia where he conducts his RITE OF SPRING and ORPHEUS ballet suite.

Van Cliburn

27-year-old **Van Cliburn** performs for two nights at Moscow's Tchaikovsky Conservatory, where he won the International Tchaikovsky Piano Competition four years ago. His recording of the First Tchaikovsky piano concerto sells one million, the first classical LP to hit that mark.

WHAT A YEAR IT WAS!

Metropolitan Opera bass **Jerome Hines**, the first American to sing the title role in Russia, receives a standing ovation at Moscow's Bolshoi Theatre for his performance as **Boris Godunov**.

Australian diva **Joan Sutherland** receives huge cheers at New York's Lewisohn Stadium at her first outdoor performance in the U.S.

She was the first black lead to sing at La Scala, the first black to play a romantic lead at the Metropolitan Opera and now brilliant coloratura **Mattiwilda Dobbs** performs before a desegregated audience of 3,000 people in Atlanta, Georgia.

The Metropolitan Opera opens its 78th season bringing new productions including **Die Meistersinger** and **Ariadne auf Naxos**.

Santa Fe Opera celebrates the 80th birthday of **Igor Stravinsky** by performing six of the composer's operas including **Oedipus Rex** and **The Rake's Progress**.

Londoners cram a concert hall to hear divine diva María Callas sing.

In West Germany on a four-city concert tour, **María Callas** is not her usual fiery self, but is charming, amiable and friendly and despite an eye infection, performs in Bonn.

María Callas receives a 15-minute standing ovation after her concert in Munich, and is so moved she gives a carnation to a woman in the audience.

Becoming the first American to sing with Russia's 110-year-old Tiflis Opera, soprano **Dorothy Kirsten** *is showered with bouquets and 22 curtain calls after performing the role of Violetta in* LA TRAVIATA.

WHAT A YEAR IT WAS!

1962 Dance

Nureyev

In September, New Yorkers spend $1 million in only three weeks to attend dance performances with the bulk being spent on the Bolshoi Ballet's second visit to the U.S. Cost of the tickets: $25 opening night (orchestra seats), $15 thereafter. The most lavish production is SPARTACUS.

Russian dancer **Rudolf Nureyev**, who defected last year in Paris from the Leningrad Kirov Ballet, makes his U.S. debut with **Ruth Page's** company at the Brooklyn Academy of Music.

After dancing Giselle, 43-year-old prima ballerina **Margot Fonteyn** calls 24-year-old **Rudolf Nureyev** one of her most satisfactory partners and says he has brought her a second career.

Nureyev is hospitalized to have a dislocated ankle bone pushed back into place.

Jose Greco, American Flamenco dancer, is knighted by the Spanish government for popularizing Spanish culture.

They're Dancin', Dancin' In The Streets

Grown-ups are dancing the Bossa Nova.

Celebrities such as **Eva Gabor** and the **Duke and Duchess of Windsor** pay $65 for six lessons from **"Killer Joe" Piro** to learn the *hully gully*, newest dance rage from Harlem to Florida.

White people flock to **Wilt Chamberlain's Big Wilt's Smalls Paradise**, a bistro in the middle of Harlem where they come to do *The Twist*.

The Ballet Russe de Monte Carlo celebrates its 25th anniversary.

The Jacob's Pillow Dance Festival holds its 30th anniversary season.

Dancers from the Metropolitan Opera Ballet give free performances for school children.

The Joffrey Ballet receives a large grant from the Rebekah Harkness Foundation to rehearse new ballets.

The American Dance Festival includes new works by **Jose Limon** (*I, Odysseus*) and **Martha Graham** (*Secular Games*).

Martha Graham and her modern dance ensemble perform two successful new works on Broadway—*Phaedra* and *A Look at Lightning*.

In a tribute to **Igor Stravinsky's** 80th birthday, CBS airs the world premiere of his *Noah and the Flood*, a dance drama narrated by **Laurence Harvey** and danced by the New York City Ballet with choreography by **George Balanchine**.

Stravinsky

George Balanchine's *A Midsummer Night's Dream*, the first original full-length American ballet, is premiered by the New York City Ballet.

WHAT A YEAR IT WAS!

Everyone's Doing The
TWIST

European bands are still blowing up a storm for The Twist.

Here's a contest for leading twisters in Germany.

All this twisting and shouting is enough to drive a chiropractor to drink.

It's dance at your own risk, as these finalists give it their all and if you're not in great shape, you'd better stay on the sidelines.

You can carry them out on the flat of their backs but they never miss a beat.

Left: Pin-striped costume with linen overblouse, about $70. Right: Textured black dress, about $65. At C. CRAWFORD HOLLIDGE

Boston • Wellesley • Hyannis

PAT SANDLER FOR HIGHLIGHT

In Canada, Jack Liebman Ltd.

1962

ON BROADWAY

RICHARD RODGERS WRITES BOTH THE LYRICS AND MUSIC FOR THE FIRST TIME FOR A BROADWAY SHOW CALLED NO STRINGS STARRING DIAHANN CARROLL AND RICHARD KILEY.

WRITING HIS FIRST BROADWAY SHOW IN 12 YEARS, IRVING BERLIN COMPOSES BOTH THE MUSIC AND LYRICS FOR MR. PRESIDENT, THE ADVANCE SALES OF WHICH ARE $1.5 MILLION THREE MONTHS BEFORE OPENING.

Nanette Fabray in
Mr. President

WHAT A YEAR IT WAS!

97

1962
ANOTHER OPENING, ANOTHER NIGHT

A Family Affair
✶
A Funny Thing Happened On The Way To The Forum
✶
A Gift Of Time
✶
A Man's A Man
✶
A Passage To India
✶
A Thousand Clowns
✶
The Affair
✶
All American
✶
The Aspern Papers
✶
The Beautiful Bait
✶
Beyond The Fringe
✶
Bravo Giovanni
✶
Brigadoon (revival)

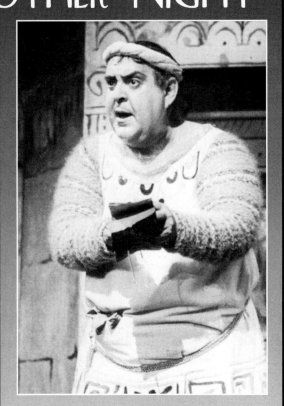

Zero Mostel in *A Funny Thing Happened On The Way To The Forum*

Calculated Risk
✶
Can Can (revival)
✶
The Captains And The Kings
✶
The Collection
✶
Come On Strong

The Dumbwaiter
✶
The Egg
✶
Fiorelllo (revival)
✶
General Seeger
✶
Giants, Son of Giants
✶
Great Day In The Morning
✶
Harold
✶
I Can Get It For You Wholesale
✶
Isle Of Children
✶
Little Me
✶
Lord Pengo
✶
Moby Dick
✶
Mr. President
✶
New Faces Of 1962
✶
Never Too Late
✶
Night Life
✶
No Strings

WHAT A YEAR IT WAS!

ANOTHER CLOSING, ANOTHER NIGHT

Nowhere To Go But Up

☆

Romulus
(adapted by Gore Vidal)

☆

Seidman And Son

☆

Step On A Crack

☆

Something About A Soldier

☆

Stop The World – I Want To Get Off

☆

Take Her, She's Mine

☆

Tchin, Tchin

☆

Venus At Large

☆

Who's Afraid Of Virginia Woolf?

Carroll Baker in *Come On Strong*

English star **Anthony Newley** brings his very successful *Stop The World—I Want To Get Off* to Broadway with *What Kind Of A Fool Am I* becoming a hit in the U.S.

Tennessee Williams premieres his new play *The Milk Train Doesn't Stop Here Anymore* in Italy and announces that he will not be writing any more plays about southern belles.

TAKE IT OFF, TAKE IT OFF, TAKE IT ALL OFF
This Was Burlesque starring **Ann Corio** is celebrating its 40th anniversary by reviving the show after a 20-year absence.

Come Blow Your Horn

☆

Do Re Mi

☆

My Fair Lady
(longest running Broadway musical closes after 2,717 performances)

☆

Purlie Victorious

☆

The Unsinkable Molly Brown

The official Broadway program

Playbill

begins a **Los Angeles** edition.

WHAT A YEAR IT WAS!

1962

OFF BROADWAY HITS

Oh Dad, Poor Dad, Mama's Hung You In The Closet And I'm Feeling So Sad
(Arthur Kopit)

Brecht On Brecht
(Theatre de Lys, Greenwich Village)

Plays For Bleeker Street
(Thornton Wilder's one-act program)

Who'll Save The Plowboy?
(Frank Gilroy)

 With Lukewarm Reviews To Boot, All Did Not End Well

Joseph Papp finally gets to produce free Shakespeare at a new $400,000 amphitheater and kicks off the New York Shakespeare Festival in Central Park with *The Merchant of Venice* which draws condemnation from the New York Board of Rabbis who protest the anti-Semitic depiction of the character Shylock.

Helen Hayes is not smiled upon by the HERALD TRIBUNE critic gods who pan her performance in *Shakespeare Revisited* performed in Stratford, Connecticut.

20-year-old **Barbra Streisand's** role of Miss Marmelstein in *I Can Get It For You Wholesale*, according to critics, is the only bargain in the Broadway musical which gets tepid reviews.

BREAKING THE COLOR BARRIERS

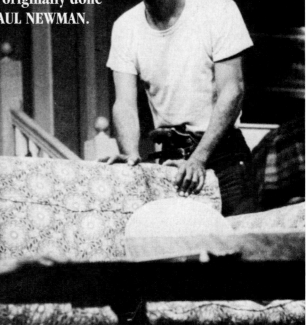

Sammy Davis, Jr. becomes one of the first blacks to perform a role written for a white lead when he stars in Long Island's Mineola Playhouse summer stock production of *The Desperate Hours*, originally done on Broadway by PAUL NEWMAN.

Singer **Dorothy Dandridge** makes her debut in a summer stock production of *West Side Story* at the Highland Park Illinois Music Theatre where she plays Anita, a Puerto Rican girl.

NOT A MUMBLER IN THE LOT

Great Britain's revered Old Vic Company arrives in the U.S. for a five-month, 13-city tour with its repertory including **Macbeth**, Shaw's **Saint Joan** and **Romeo And Juliet**, which is being directed by a young Italian named Franco Zeffirelli who designs stunning sets depicting Verona.

CAN'T BUILD A BETTER MOUSETRAP THAN THIS

71-year-old Agatha Christie's **The Mousetrap** is in its tenth year on a West End stage in London.

WHO SAYS IT'S THE CULTURAL ANUS OF THE COUNTRY??

Los Angeles is the nation's second largest theatrical center with more than 40 theatres in active operation, many of which are hosting road companies performing successful Broadway plays.

IF HE ONLY HAD A HIT

David Merrick announces he will be bringing the British musical **Oliver** to L.A.'s Philharmonic Auditorium for its pre-New York opening.

 WHAT A YEAR IT WAS!

Tony Awards
1962

PLAY
"A Man For All Seasons"
Robert Bolt (playwright)

MUSICAL
"How To Succeed In Business Without Really Trying"
Abe Burrows & Frank Loesser

DRAMATIC ACTOR
Paul Scofield
"A Man For All Seasons"

DRAMATIC ACTRESS
Margaret Leighton
"Night Of The Iguana"

COMPOSER
Richard Rodgers
"No Strings"

MUSICAL ACTOR
Robert Morse
"How To Succeed In Business Without Really Trying"

MUSICAL ACTRESS (tie)
Anna Maria Alberghetti
"Carnival"

Diahann Carroll
"No Strings"

NEW YORK DRAMA CRITICS' CIRCLE AWARD

BEST AMERICAN PLAY	THE NIGHT OF THE IGUANA
BEST FOREIGN PLAY	A MAN FOR ALL SEASONS
BEST MUSICAL	HOW TO SUCCEED IN BUSINESS WITHOUT REALLY TRYING

SPECIAL AWARDS

Brooks Atkinson
Richard Rodgers
Franco Zeffirelli

Pulitzer Prize for Drama
How To Succeed In Business Without Really Trying
Frank Loesser & Abe Burrows

HOW DOES BETTY MEASURE UP? 37-24-35

46-year-old World War II pin-up **Betty Grable** stars in a new Las Vegas production of *Guys And Dolls*.

After a week of rehearsing for her Broadway debut in a stage play, 43-year-old screen star **Rita Hayworth** drops out of *Step On A Crack* saying she is too physically and emotionally exhausted to keep her commitment.

15-year-old **Patty Duke**, whose portrayal of Helen Keller in the Broadway production of *The Miracle Worker* brought her instant fame, has a starring role in *Isle Of Children* which is her first speaking part onstage.

FAMOUS BIRTH
Matthew Broderick

WHAT A YEAR IT WAS!

101

Oldsmobile Division • General Motors Corp.

Where the joy of driving meets pride of ownership!

Driving's a rare treat when you slide *this* beauty into action! For the stunning new '63 Oldsmobile surrounds you with cushioned, carpeted luxury. Its spirited, responsive V-8 performance is complemented by a comfortable coil-spring ride.

Add to that the kind of trend-setting style that makes you proud you chose Oldsmobile! Drive one today! Let it tell you all you need to know about fine automobiles! And let your Oldsmobile Dealer show you how little it costs to own one!

There's "Something Extra" about owning an

OLDSMOBILE

NINETY-EIGHT • SUPER 88 • DYNAMIC 88 • F-85 • STARFIRE • JETFIRE

102

At The MUSEUM

1962

The American Association of Museums releases a statement that a museum is "…open to the public, and administered in the public interest, for the purpose of conserving and preserving, studying, interpreting, assembling and exhibiting to the public for its instruction and enjoyment of objects and specimens of educational and cultural value…"

Paintings by **Gauguin**, **Monet**, **Manet**, **Leger** and **Renoir** are seen at Brandeis University's new *Rose Art Museum*.

A Robert Motherwell exhibit at the **Pasadena Museum** features the 17½-foot long "The Voyage, Ten Years After."

Robert Motherwell

ART

NeW YoRK PoP ArT

Junk food inspires CLAES OLDENBURG, and his enormous replicas of cake, a hamburger topped by a pickle and an ice cream cone are on view at Green Gallery.

Oldenburg continues holding his "Happenings," performance pieces where art meets theatre.

ANDY WARHOL's homage to Marilyn Monroe, 20 similar but different images, and some of his Campbell's Soup cans are on view at Stable Gallery.

Andy Warhol

ROY LICHTENSTEIN paints "Blam" and has a one-man show at Castelli Gallery. Included is a picture of an oversized golf ball.

1962

NEW YORK
The Big Apple

Young California painter **EDWARD MOSES** has his first New York City show.

HENRY MOORE is commissioned to create a sculpture for Lincoln Center.

A **JEAN DUBUFFET** retrospective at MOMA includes 185 sculptures, assemblages, paintings and drawings.

MOMA's **"Design For Sport"** show features sports equipment from around the world.

PAUL KLEE's son lends 42 never-before-seen canvases to E. and A. Silberman Galleries.

LOUISE NEVELSON becomes the first woman represented by the exclusive Sidney Janis Gallery.

GEORGIA O'KEEFFE is elected to the **National Academy Of Arts and Letters.**

Calder

FEEL ME, TOUCH ME

The largest Alexander Calder retrospective to date is on view at London's Tate Gallery where thousands of visitors are encouraged to touch his mobiles.

The Museum of the City of New York inaugurates a kid's room entitled **"Please Touch."**

Jackson Pollock

paintings and sketchbooks are on view at the Wadsworth Atheneum in Hartford, Connecticut.

ACQUISITIONS

The **ANDREW WYETH** canvas *"That Gentleman"* is bought by the Dallas Museum of Fine Arts for $58,000, the most ever paid for a living American painter. In Buffalo, New York over 140 pieces are shown during a Wyeth retrospective.

Works of art costing about $100 are now available from **Sears, Roebuck & Co.**, which hires actor **Vincent Price** to find affordable pieces.

$$ KA-CHING $$

Matisse
"Interior With Yellow Chair"
$106,000

Monet
"Nympheas"
$200,000

Renoir
"Three Girls Walking"
$134,400

Modigliani
"Man With Glass Of Wine"
$103,600

Degas
nude
$211,000

Van Gogh
"Still Life With Oranges, Lemons And Blue Gloves"
$224,000

WHAT A YEAR IT WAS!

LONDON

J. Paul Getty purchases Rembrandt's "St. Bartholomew" at a London auction for $532,000.

Queen Elizabeth shares the Royals' private, centuries-old collection with the public by opening the Queen's Gallery, located at Buckingham Palace.

Scotland Yard recovers 35 stolen paintings worth $1.2 million including works by Picasso, Toulouse-Lautrec, Monet and Renoir.

The British Government and the public join forces to raise $2,240,000 to insure Leonardo da Vinci's "Virgin and Child with St. Anne and St. John the Baptist" stays in the country. It is the second highest price ever paid for a work of art.

Pope John XXIII *agrees to loan Michelangelo's marble "Pieta" to the 1964 New York World's Fair. The one-ton statue has never left the Vatican and is the artist's only signed sculpture.*

Alberto Giacometti wins the top sculpture prize at the 31st Venice Biennale. Louise Nevelson and Arshile Gorky are featured in the U.S. pavilion.

Leonardo da Vinci's "Mona Lisa" arrives in the U.S. by boat from France for a special exhibit and is protected by surveillance cameras, guards and thermostats that monitor temperature and humidity.

"Treasures of Versailles" opens a new wing of the Art Institute of Chicago. The show, with pieces from the time of Louis XIV onward, including a tiara worn by Empress Josephine, travels to several museums across the country.

1962

A CUBIST EXHIBIT AT PARIS' KNOEDLER GALLERY FEATURES PIECES BY PICASSO, GRIS, LEGER AND BRAQUE.

Picasso

Pablo Picasso's 80th birthday (October 1961) is celebrated throughout the year with special events:

At the Worcester Art Museum an exhibit featuring works from 1938-1961 includes *"Portrait Of Dora Maar."*

A Picasso is sold from W. Somerset Maugham's collection for $224,000, a record price for a living artist. The painting is unique in that it has *"The Death Of Harlequin"* on the front combined with *"Woman In A Garden"* on the back.

Nine Manhattan galleries participate in *"Picasso – An American Tribute."* Each gallery displays one stage, time period or medium of the master's work. Over 300 drawings, paintings and sculpture make up the comprehensive month-long exhibition which is seen by 140,000 people.

PICASSO DECLARES TWO OF HIS SUPPOSED PAINTINGS IN THE WALTER P. CHRYSLER, JR. COLLECTION ARE FAKES.

"Guernica" is one of several dozen pieces on view at MOMA.

A few *"Bathers"* arrive at the Museum of Fine Arts in Houston and are displayed in and around a pool built especially for the Picasso sculptures.

The Guggenheim...

Guggenheim Museum

... displays its complete sculpture collection for the first time, featuring pieces by CALDER, BRANCUSI, ARP, GIACOMETTI, DUCHAMP-VILLON, NOGUCHI and MODIGLIANI.

... has a LEGER exhibit and acquires his "The Great Parade."

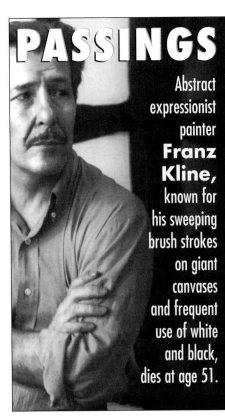

PASSINGS

Abstract expressionist painter **Franz Kline,** known for his sweeping brush strokes on giant canvases and frequent use of white and black, dies at age 51.

JACKIE KENNEDY BECOMES A TRUSTEE FOR WASHINGTON'S NATIONAL GALLERY OF ART. A **FRANZ KLINE** SHOW INAUGURATES THE NEW MUSEUM.

ARCHITECTURE
+DESIGN

Eero Saarinen

posthumously receives the American Institute of Architects' Gold Medal and the Medal of Honor from the AIA's New York division.

Work begins on the last building, and only skyscraper, designed by Saarinen. The new Midtown Manhattan headquarters for CBS will rise from a sunken plaza, reach 38 stories and be fabricated of concrete and dark granite.

COME FLY WITH ME

Saarinen is responsible for the latest in airport news. His $15 million TWA terminal at New York's Idlewild opens, with soaring lines and an expansive feel resembling the freedom of a flying bird. A similar sense of openness is built into his design at Dulles International Airport, located in a Virginia suburb just outside Washington, D.C. Saarinen-created mobile lounges transport passengers comfortably from terminals to planes, keeping them warm in the winter and cool in the summer. President Kennedy participates in the airport's dedication ceremony.

The Kaufman International Design Award goes to Bauhaus founder Walter Gropius.

1962

In a newly renovated section of Philadelphia, over two dozen I.M. Pei-designed town homes are built.

Le Corbusier's government building in Punjab, India is completed while his visual arts center is under construction at Harvard.

PHILIP JOHNSON

Ground is broken for an addition to the Museum of Modern Art, designed by Philip Johnson. Included will be a revamped and enlarged garden with sculpture scattered throughout.

Johnson is hired by Israel's Minister of Defense Shimon Peres to design a structure to store a nuclear reactor.

ON THE INSIDE

With the strong influence of Jackie Kennedy and her ongoing restoration of the White House, lots of Americans are inspired to try their hand at interior design.

Approximately 6 1/2 million American homes are air-conditioned.

Apartment buildings account for nearly 30 percent of new housing starts.

FURNITURE

Solid, embellished furniture with a Mediterranean flavor and the sleek Modern look are popular styles.

Elder Americans favor Modern furniture when decorating their homes.

WHAT A YEAR IT WAS!

108

County Museum of Art, Los Angeles
Architect – **William Pereira Associates**

c Center, Los Angeles
tect – **Welton Becket & Associates**

Marin County Civic Center, San Rafael
Architect – **Frank Lloyd Wright**

The 50-story
Hotel Americana
opens in Manhattan, instantly
becoming the highest hotel
in the world.

THE **New York Hilton**
is under construction.

For the hotel guest who wants
everything, Chicago's
O'Hare Inn
has added a bomb shelter in
addition to lots of new rooms.

PASSINGS

Famed builder of the mass-
developed Levittown communities
in New York, New Jersey and
Pennsylvania, Abraham Levitt,
patriarch of Levitt & Sons, dies
at age 82.

Co-founder of Skidmore,
Owings & Merrill, the biggest
architectural firm in America,
revolutionary modern architect
Louis Skidmore dies at age 65.

WHAT A YEAR IT WAS!

for rooms with a colorful personality... choose ready-mades from the Chromspun "House of Color"

Lawrence Peabody, AID, blends modern with traditional accessories to give this room its individual charm. Its focal point? The glowing richness of ready-mades from the Chromspun "House of Color." Bedspreads, bed pillows and draperies are in a subtly textured weave of 100% Chromspun acetate. Like the floor cushions and furniture, they're beautiful examples of the fine furnishings you find in better stores when you look for the Chromspun "House of Color" symbol. It takes the guesswork out of decorating, because Chromspun hues are color-locked against fading...color-linked to match or harmonize perfectly.

Bedspread, bed pillows and draperies by Nettle Creek of 100% Chromspun acetate. Avocado, Peacock, Pink, Red, Melon, Gold, Beige, Purple, Teal, White. Single bedspread, about $40; double, about $50; dual, about $60. Single-width draperies, 90" long, unlined, about $16. Pillows, according to size and style. *For store nearest you, write Nettle Creek Industries, Dept. B-10, Richmond, Ind.* Furniture designed by Lawrence Peabody for Richardson Nemschoff. The patterned glass by American-St. Gobain.

Chromspun is the trademark for Eastman color-locked acetate fiber. Only fiber is made by Eastman, not fabrics or furnishings.

CHROMSPUN ®

EASTMAN CHEMICAL PRODUCTS, INC., *subsidiary of Eastman Kodak Company,* 260 MADISON AVE., NEW YORK 16

Books

Robert Frost RECEIVES Congressional Medal

President Kennedy presents him with the Congressional Medal in recognition of his contribution to U.S. literature. President Kennedy remarks that it was a unanimous vote by Congress, adding that it was the only thing they've been able to agree on for a long time.

Celebrating his 88th birthday, Robert Frost, the grand old man of American letters, is honored by the White House.

In return, Mr. Frost presents Mr. Kennedy with a copy of his latest book, *IN THE CLEARING*. Asked if he thinks this might be his last book, the outspoken poet says he hopes his wits last a little longer, but warns that one of these days he may say something foolish.

NEVER TOO OLD TO MISS YOUR MOMMY

On receiving the MacDowell Colony Medal from the Academy of American Poets, poet **Robert Frost** quips that he wishes his mother could see him now.

James Joyce is finally given proper recognition in his hometown of Dublin. A celebration begins on June 16, the day on which his masterpiece "Ulysses" is set. Festivities include the dedication of a James Joyce museum, a theatrical presentation of "Ulysses" and a fashion show.

JAMES JOYCE, the Dubliner

1962 Books

A Bridge For Passing
Pearl S. Buck

A Clockwork Orange
Anthony Burgess

A Shade Of Difference
Allen Drury

A Wrinkle In Time
Madeleine L'Engle

The Age Of Happy Problems
Herbert Gold

An Unofficial Rose
Iris Murdoch

Another Country
James Baldwin

The Big Laugh
John O'Hara

Big Sur
Jack Kerouac

Book Of Common Sense Etiquette
Eleanor Roosevelt

Dearly Beloved
Anne Morrow Lindbergh

Deaths For The Ladies
And Other Disasters
Norman Mailer

Down There On A Visit
Christopher Isherwood

Dr. Seuss's Sleep Book
Theodor "Dr. Seuss" Geisel

The Drowned World
J.G. Ballard

The Dyer's Hand
And Other Essays
W.H. Auden

Fail-Safe
Eugene Burdick and Harvey Wheeler

The Golden Notebook
Doris Lessing

The Gutenberg Galaxy; The
Making Of Typographic Man
Marshall McLuhan

High In The Thin Cold Air
Sir Edmund Hillary & Desmond Doig

In The Clearing
Robert Frost

Island
Aldous Huxley

It's A Battlefield
Graham Greene

The Joyous Cosmology
Alan Watts

Just Friends
And Brave Enemies
Robert F. Kennedy

Labyrinths
Jorge Luis Borges

Letting Go
Philip Roth

The Lonely Life
Bette Davis

The Man In The High Castle
Philip K. Dick

Marlene Dietrich's ABC

Mr. Wilson's War
John Dos Passos

My Land And My People
Dalai Lama

One Day In The Life
Of Ivan Denisovich
Alexander Solzhenitsyn

PRIZES

NOBEL

Literature
JOHN STEINBECK, USA

PULITZER

Public Service
Panama City News-Herald

National Reporting
NATHAN G.
CALDWELL &
GENE S. GRAHAM

*Nashville
Tennessean*

International Reporting
WALTER
LIPPMAN

*New York
Herald Tribune
Syndicate*

Editorial Writing
THOMAS M.
STORKE

*Santa Barbara
News-Press*

Editorial Cartooning
EDMUND S.
VALTMAN

*Hartford
Times*

Photography
PAUL VATHIS
AP

Fiction
EDWIN O'CONNOR
"The Edge Of Sadness"

History
LAWRENCE H. GIPSON
**"The Triumphant Empire:
Thunder-Clouds Gather In
The West 1763-1766"**

Poetry
ALAN DUGAN
"Poems"

Nonfiction
THEODORE H. WHITE
**"The Making Of The
President, 1960"**

PASSINGS

Poet **e e cummings**, whose penchant for lower case letters and imaginative punctuation added to his uniqueness, dies at age 67.

Baroness Karen Blixen, better known as **Isak Dinesen** who wrote "Out of Africa" and other tales inspired by her time living in Kenya, dies at age 76.

Mississippi native, Nobel and Pulitzer Prize winner and former whisky runner **William Faulkner** dies at age 64, leaving behind such notable works as "The Sound and the Fury," "A Fable" and "As I Lay Dying."

Pacifist and Nobel prize-winning author of such classics as "Steppenwolf" and "Siddhartha," **Hermann Hesse** dies at age 85.

Author of "The Joy of Cooking," which has sold over six million copies worldwide, **Irma Rombauer** dies at age 83.

One Flew Over The Cuckoo's Nest
Ken Kesey

The Other America
Michael Harrington

Pale Fire
Vladimir Nabokov

Pigeon Feathers And Other Stories
John Updike

The Prime Of Life
Simone de Beauvoir

The Prize
Irving Wallace

The Reivers
William Faulkner

Renoir, My Father
Jean Renoir

Rocking The Boat
Gore Vidal

The San Franciscans
Niven Busch

Sex And The Single Girl
Helen Gurley Brown

Ship Of Fools
Katherine Anne Porter

Silent Spring
Rachel Carson

 Perhaps with a bit of psychic accuracy, **OGDEN NASH** declares his famous **"Candy is dandy, but liquor is quicker"** couplet will be the only thing people will remember long after his passing.

The Slave
Isaac Bashevis Singer

The Spy Who Loved Me
Ian Fleming

Stand Still Like The Hummingbird
Henry Miller

Tale For The Mirror
Hortense Calisher

The Thin Red Line
James Jones

The Tin Drum
(translated into English)
Gunther Grass

To Turn The Tide
President John F. Kennedy

Travels With Charley
John Steinbeck

We Seven
The Astronauts Themselves

Where Has Love Gone
Harold Robbins

Wolf Willow
Wallace Stegner

The Wonderful Clouds
Francoise Sagan

Youngblood Hawke
Herman Wouk

NATIONAL BOOK AWARDS

Fiction

"The Moviegoer"
Walker Percy

Poetry

"The City In History"
Lewis Mumford

1962

MAD magazine celebrates its 10th anniversary.

Harper & Row

is created as Row, Peterson & Co. merges with Harper & Bros.

Dartmouth names a section of its library for America's beloved poet, **Robert Frost**. His contemporary **Carl Sandburg**, the poet with the *"little cat feet,"* becomes Illinois' poet laureate.

"Poetry" magazine turns 50.

The first **National Poetry Festival** is put on by the Library of Congress.

"The White House: An Historic Guide," with an introduction by First Lady Jackie Kennedy, uses both vivid photos and text to share the history of the most famous house in the nation.

William Faulkner receives the GOLD MEDAL from the American Academy of Arts and Letters.

William Burrough's 1959 *"Naked Lunch,"* written in a free-form, cut-up style, is finally published in the United States while **Henry Miller**'s *"Tropic of Capricorn,"* originally published in Paris in 1939, is finally printed in America.

MODERN MASTERS BOOKS FOR CHILDREN enlists the services of such renowned authors, poets and playwrights as **William Saroyan**, **Arthur Miller**, **Mark Van Doren** and **Phyllis McGinley** to write some interesting prose for youngsters.

Some changes in the newest edition of the **Dick and Jane** series include modern plots and pictures as well as an increased and more contemporary vocabulary.

Mary **H**emingway shuffles through some personal effects of her late husband Ernest stored in a Florida bar and finds sections of original drafts of "Death In The Afternoon" and "To Have And Have Not."

WHAT A YEAR IT WAS!

FASHION — 1962

Oh, Jackie

Oleg Cassini continues to be Jackie's designer of choice, and creates stunning and colorful outfits for her visit to India. One favorite—a sleeveless silk apricot v-neck dress with a bow at the waist worn with white gloves and pearls. Designers are inspired by Jackie's trip and begin using luscious Indian fabrics and styles.

Jackie wears evening gowns to White House affairs including a pleated sea-green silk jersey Cassini worn to a Nobel Prize Laureate function and a strapless pink Dior worn while entertaining France's Minister of Culture, Andre Malraux.

Her inaugural gown, a long white chiffon dress topped by an embroidered silver camisole and long gloves, is added to the Smithsonian's First Ladies' Hall.

She is voted one of the ten best-coiffed women of the year.

When Jackie wears a bow in her hair to a public event much of the U.S. female population follows suit.

Jackie's penchant for wraparound sunglasses starts a national craze.

1962
London Designers
Display Newest Fashions

Major London designers mark fashion week with a showing of autumn fashions that indicate a resurgence of daring among Britain's stylists. This semi-fitted polished worsted suit and leather hat is aimed at the over 30 trade.

This short dress and jacket are made from the famous British Lieber's lace, a fine fabric for dresses and light coats.

You'll enjoy country living in this wool sweater dress with black ribbed polo collar and cuffs.

Then out of country clothes and into this strapless satin evening gown for a night on the town. From the classic suit to flimsy eveningwear, London stylists have special designs for the ladies.

WHAT A YEAR IT WAS!

Across The Atlantic

Princess Margaret continues to be one of Britain's most stylish women. Her ancient Greek-inspired hairdo has tongues a-wagging as to whether all the hair belongs to Her Royal Highness or if she has a little bit of wig help. The London fashion press isn't wild about Margaret riding on a motorcycle in a skirt or her one-strap evening gown.

According to Britain's "Tailor & Cutter," some world leaders who could use a world-class makeover include **Kennedy, Khrushchev, de Gaulle** *and* **Castro.**

Castro: fashion victim?

A $3,400 ruby and diamond brooch depicting an A-bomb blast wins Britain's Jewel of the Year award.

WHAT A YEAR IT WAS!

Vive la France 1962

WHAT'S IN *in Paris*

- Backless And Slim Evening Dresses
  - Belts Cinching The Waist Tightly
- Bows And Ruffles
- Capes
- Colorful Print Blouses
- Crepe
- Culottes
- Fitted Garments
- Glitter
- Lace Up Shoes
- Large Jet Jewelry
- Lush Fabrics Such As Silk, Lace And Brocade
- Shawls
- Shirtwaist Dresses
- Skirts Below The Knee, With And Without Pleats
- Suits Made Of Organza, Faille Or Linen With Hip-Hitting Jackets
- Tweed
- Two-Piece Dresses

The House of Dior makes fashionable apparel for young ladies.

Italian designer **Roberto Capucci** *opens his couture house in Paris.*

YVES ST. LAURENT

Yves St. Laurent *opens his own house of fashion to thunderous approval from haute couture fans. Some St. Laurent offerings include a tweed suit in black and beige, a silk overblouse, a tunic dress, a crepe evening dress and the instantly successful pea-jacket coat. He tops it all off with an updated Babushka-style hat.*

The Paris fashion world is all aflutter when the **House of Dior** *files a lawsuit against* **Yves St. Laurent** *charging him with stealing valuable Dior employees. St. Laurent denies the charges.*

COCOLOCO
The latest incarnation of the classic Chanel suit features huge houndstooth checks and cashmere trim.

1962

In Your EASTER BONNETS

*N*ext to the circus, what better sign of spring than Easter bonnets as evidenced by these factory women hard at work sewing the season's favorites.

*T*he hats are being readied for the big parade.

*T*he flowered and bowed number contrasts nicely with the organdy.

*H*ere's a large brimmed cloche in silk print.

*O*r maybe you prefer a shiny straw Breton banded with grosgrain ribbon.

*T*his companion piece is sprinkled with apple blossoms.

WHAT A YEAR IT WAS!

HATS

*H*ere's a straw beret with decorative bow.

*C*ompletely flowered for complete flattery, poppies form this chic cloche.

*A*nd to top this tale of toppers, here's an oversized flounce brim with a flower playing peek-a-boo.

*A*s the bands are tuning up for the Easter Parade this year, the ladies can be sure they will have a hat full of style.

Hats add drama, from the smallest turban to the largest straw, and are worn day or night. Other popular styles include the fedora, beret, boater and anything soft and feathery. Wide and high hats fit nicely over shorter hairdos.

WHAT A YEAR IT WAS!

1962

SHOES

Lightweight shoes, often constructed of man-made materials, are supremely comfortable.

Boots are ankle-length, knee-length or anywhere in between.

Low heels are key in every design for playing, walking and even dressing up.

Opera pumps and sling-backs work best for fancy occasions.

The simple, comfortable "shift" dress takes center stage in the fashion spotlight and becomes the perfect little garment for every age and every occasion.

Seamless stockings guaranteed to be run-proof hit the stores.

COLOR MY WORLD

SMOKY GREY is the hot color for fall.

You can't go wrong wearing *Turquoise, Topaz, Garnet, Fuchsia, Plum, Navy, Mauve, Brown, Scarlet, Beige, Red, Orange, Mulberry, Amber, Ruby, Claret* or *Pewter.*

Oversized **CHECKS** and **PLAIDS** may be dizzying, yet they are dazzling and a great choice for suits and dresses.

BLACK, WHITE *or* **BLACK** *with* WHITE *is au courant.*

Zebra stripes contribute to this trend.

120

WHAT A YEAR IT WAS!

The look-again look!

Ban-Lon® Warp Knit fabric

mort schrader designs a living fashion with built-in elegance and ease, because it's made of "Ban-Lon" Warp Knit fabric by Maxwell. The case for this now-famous fabric rests in its uniquely crimped "Textralized" yarn. This assures soft-as-silk luxury and the ability to outwit wrinkling and stretching. Slender afternoon dress with cap sleeves, draped neckline, velvet belt. Turquoise on white; 6-16 petites; 100% Nylon; about $45. At Lord & Taylor, New York; Filene's, Boston; Chas. A. Stevens & Co., Chicago; Rich's, Atlanta; J. W. Robinson Co., Los Angeles.

"Everglaze" Marketing Division, Wilmington, Delaware, supervises the international merchandising of products approved to carry the Joseph Bancroft & Sons Co. trademarks "Ban-Lon" and/or "Everglaze"

1962 FROM THE SOVIET BLOC COUNTRIES

Top stylists from nine countries compete for the Coiffeur Championship of the World, Eastern Division.

Let's see what's back here.

Spectators are fascinated.

And here's some heady looks for the men.

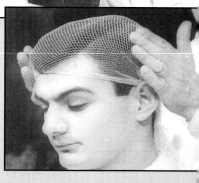

How would you go about netting this guy?

Just a little snip here and there. It doesn't take 'em long to root out the amateurs. Come now comrade, this reflects the decadent west.

Voila!

The finished look.

Whoops!

He may have snipped a bit too much.

WHAT A YEAR IT WAS!

S

It takes a long hard look to decide on the winners.

And here are the winners. (Believe it or not!)

1962

It's Wiggy, Man

Wigs are all the rage with women in the U.S. who jam stores across the nation for synthetic wigs or their more costly human hair counterparts. Saks Fifth Avenue offers an aqua wig, waterproof manufactured hair with a bathing cap underneath to protect ladies' real manes. "Falls," lacquered to perfection hair pieces that fall from the top of the head, are another way for a woman to temporarily change her look.

Goodbye Oversized Beehives, Hello Soft, Flowing Locks

Hairstyles are simpler and more natural looking than previous seasons.

1962

CLICK CLICK

Photographer **Richard Avedon's** photo of model **Christina Paolozzi**, nude from the waist up, is published in **Harper's Bazaar**.

Shortly before her death, **Marilyn Monroe** does a fashion shoot for **Vogue**.

After 27 years at **Harper's Bazaar**, **Diana Vreeland** becomes associate editor of **Vogue**.

HALSTON wins a **Coty award** for his outstanding contribution to the fashion industry.

COURTING NEW WEAR

The new rule at Wimbledon is white undies for all.

California sportswear designer **Rudi Gernreich** predicts in the near future American women will wear topless bathing suits. In the meantime, his newest bikini line is filled with skimpy shapes and geometric patterns.

Cinema influences the fashion world. **CLEOPATRA** takes designers back a few centuries for slim gowns and big jewelry while *Breakfast at Tiffany's* popularizes the princess dress.

J.C. Penney's sells **Mary Quant** dresses for $20.

Norman Norell is the #1 designer in America and his spring suit is knocked off by copycats throughout the country.

According to **Mr. Blackwell**, some of the **WORLD'S WORST-DRESSED WOMEN** include Lucille Ball, Brigitte Bardot, Ingrid Bergman, Bette Davis, Zsa Zsa Gabor, Judy Garland, Pat Lawford, Rosalind Russell and Dinah Shore.

Bergman

THE BEST-DRESSED LADIES IN THE WORLD

Jackie Kennedy (#1 for three years)
Princess Lee Radziwill
Princess Sirikit of Thailand
Gloria Vanderbilt
Joan Crawford
Audrey Hepburn
Irene Dunne
Doris Day
Dina Merrill
Vivian Blaine

Hepburn

WHAT A YEAR IT WAS!

New PRODUCTS 1962 and INVENTIONS

Soldiers Walk On Water

Pentagon officials review the latest equipment designed to make the foot soldier more flexible.

Each shoe weighs seven pounds and is capable of supporting 350 pounds. The inventors envision its use by soldiers when water is too deep for wading.

Five feet of buoyant foam that enable an infantryman to forge streams and swampy terrain.

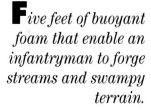

But the boots will no doubt be put to more immediate use at beaches and lakes as there are all sorts of possibilities as demonstrated by these lovely ladies.

It's a water hauling apparatus

In Germany it's called the **wasserschleppgerat**, a self-propelled boat equipped with throttle-control handlebars that allows a water skier to drive himself at speeds of up to 25 mph.

1962

To cut down on the glare of headlights during night driving, the new two-position **Glare Guard**, which either clips on your eyeglasses or can be worn on frames of their own, is available for **$6.95-$8.95**.

No More Shattering Experiences?

CORNING GLASS WORKS invents a new process called *Chemcor*, which tempers glass chemically making it up to five times stronger than any previous known glass.

ON A SHORT FUSE?

Don't know which fuse blew? Well, now look for the one with the purplish, fluorescent glow, which will continue for ten minutes after it blows.

Make Mine Six Carats, Please

General Electric Company has developed a laser light beam that can cut fine holes in diamonds.

BUCKLE EVERYONE UP FOR SAFETY

To protect your youngster in the car you can now put him in a new molded car seat with its own seat belt, locked into the car by using the car's safety belt.

Actress **Hedy Lamarr** and **George Antheil** secure a patent for their anti-jamming device called *frequency hopping*.

THE WORLD'S MOST POWERFUL AIRLINER, THE VICKERS VC-10 WITH A ROLLS-ROYCE ENGINE AND 151 PASSENGER CAPACITY, ROLLS OUT OF ITS HANGAR AT WEYBRIDGE, ENGLAND.

HOPE THIS IS NOT A SHOCKING EXPERIENCE

Stuart Motors of Kalamazoo, Michigan introduces its *Stuart*, an electric car powered by lead acid storage batteries.

ALL THIS AND NO SICK DAYS

Touting it as one of the most important new products the company ever developed, **IBM** introduces a computer designed for small and medium size businesses with programs for payroll, sales and billing.

The *DESTROYIT SUPER-SPEED*, a paper shredder the size of a typewriter and capable of shredding up to 500 pounds of paper per hour, is available from **Michael Lith Sales Corp. of Manhattan**.

TRASH *IN* FERTILIZER *OUT*

An experimental plant in the Los Angeles area sponsored by **Lockheed Aircraft** is turning garbage into marketable products.

WHAT A YEAR IT WAS!

GETTING A NEW BUZZ ON THINGS

An easy to install pocket paging system that operates on radio frequencies has been developed by Multitone Electronics, Ltd.

Bell Telephone is offering a handset with volume control for people with impaired hearing.

A Musical Interlude

Melody Phone of Coral Gables, Florida is manufacturing a musical telephone attachment to keep you amused while you're waiting to be connected.

Calling
Dick Tracy

Cartoonist Chester Gould develops a real two-way wrist radio based on his comic strip version which sends messages up to 700 ft. and can be yours for only **$27.**

FASTER THAN A SPEEDING FINGER

Faster than dial phones and capable of transferring incoming calls to another number, the ten button push-button phones go into commercial use.

blah...blah...

ONE MORE WORD OUT OF YOU AND I'LL SCREAM

Using a built-in record player with replaceable records and batteries, a new doll called *Chatterbox* recites almost 50 words when you press her button.

WHAT'S NEXT? FOOT FREE?

AC Spark Plug has developed a new hands-free car phone which uses a small boom-type microphone and a foot switch.

THE SOUND OF CRUNCHING POTATO CHIPS?

SLUMBER TONE, a new device that emits a comforting sound thought to be the same as what the baby hears in the womb, is attached to the crib or carriage where it will lull your little darling to sleep.

STOCK UP ON THOSE DIMES

All across America, **American Telephone & Telegraph** will be replacing its 1.1 million black three-coin slot pay phones with a new two-tone one-coin slot and phase out all the old phones by 1964.

BEING A MAN OF **FEW** WORDS WOULD HELP

RCA has developed a dictating device that will print your words on paper provided you stick to its present 100-word vocabulary capability.

1962

Just When You Thought You Couldn't Keep Your Beer Cold

An 18-pound portable electric refrigerator that plugs into your car lighter is being offered by the **Otto Bernz Co.** of Rochester, New York as a lightweight luxury item for boating, fishing, hunting, camping, picnics and house trailers.

ON THE CUTTING EDGE

American Safety Razor Corp. is marketing a new stainless steel adjustable injector razor with a comfort control dial for $1.95.

With a selling price of $.23, a throw-away polyethylene umbrella is being sold on the streets of Seoul, South Korea.

bubbling over with ease

In the first major design change since coin meters were affixed to laundry appliances 30 years ago, **Maytag** develops the first self-service commercial washer which uses a plastic ticket instead of a coin to activate the machine.

WURLITZER CO. has developed a battery-powered, lightweight, electronic piano so when you go to the beach or on a picnic you can now bring along your own music.

JAPAN'S SONY HAS INTRODUCED MICRO-TV, A MINIATURE PORTABLE TELEVISION SET WITH A SCREEN SMALLER THAN A POSTCARD.

TAN in a CAN

New instant tanning lotions hit the market, which give the skin a sun glow instantly.

CASTING AROUND FOR A CAST

Mine Safety Appliances Co. has brought out an instant splint which can be inflated like a balloon and immobilize a broken limb until it can be put in a cast.

A SHOCKING EXPERIENCE

Dr. William B. Kouwenhoven of Johns Hopkins University has invented a portable electrical device called the *DEFIBRILLATOR* which can be used in cases involving ventricular fibrillation caused by electric shock.

DON'T FORGET YOUR EARPLUGS & GOGGLES

Skin diver Sam Raymond of Watertown, Massachusetts has invented a waterproof plastic camera case making it possible to take pictures underwater with the Polaroid Land Camera.

SOMETHING TO IMMERSE YOURSELVES IN TOGETHER

A miniature submarine built for two has been created by Rigsby Underwater Services and will retail for about $4,000.

POLAROID INTRODUCES COLOR FILM WITH A ONE-MINUTE DEVELOPING TIME

POINT, AIM AND CLICK

For $139 you can buy a camera that sets itself, has an electronic flash and comes loaded with a color film magazine.

The world's first slide projector with a built-in sound recording and playback system is being marketed by Revere Camera Co.

PUTTING A BETTER SPIN ON THE VINYL

Armour Industrial Chemical Co. of Chicago has invented an anti-static material designed to bring longer life and better sound fidelity to phonograph records.

WHAT A YEAR IT WAS!

There's a new soda kid in town called Sprite from Coca-Cola.

1962

ARE THEY OFF THEIR ROCK-ERS?

Bloomingdale's answer to New York Scotch drinkers who don't want chlorinated water on their rocks is *ScotcH2O*, bottled water imported from Scotland and selling for $.22 each.

CAN OPENERS AWAY!

The packaging industry is using a newly-developed can with a "pull-top" for easy opening.

TWIST AND LIFT

Having trouble opening a bottle? You can now use the new *Twist-Off*, a tear-shaped ring of rubber that gives you the extra grip and leverage you need to get that cap off.

They've Said A Mouthful

In answer to the not-so-great taste of the diet aid Metrecal, Mead Johnson & Co. is coming out with Metrecal soup in three flavors — cream of tomato, clam chowder and split pea with ham which will cost $.39 for a 225-calorie meal.

How Sweet It Is — But Oh That Aftertaste

Sweetened with cyclamates, Royal Crown Cola puts out Diet Rite Cola, the first sugar-free cola.

HAVE MIXER, WILL TRAVEL

Sunbeam puts out the first battery powered hand mixer.

NOW HOW DID THEY GET THE YOLK INTO THE BOTTLE WITHOUT BREAKING IT ?
Fresh, bottled eggs are being test marketed in supermarkets across the country.

Kookies & Kakes For Kids

Using a light bulb to bake a tiny cake or cookies, Kenner Products presents the EASY-BAKE OVEN for kids.

FRY & TOSS

From Sterno, the makers of canned heat, now comes **Disposa-Pans**, 10-inch aluminum disposable frying pans.

BRINGING HOME THE BACON—INSTANTLY

Chicago's Armour & Co. offers housewives instant bacon for the first time which cooks in three minutes vs. nine to twelve minutes for regular bacon.

MINNESOTA MINING & MANUFACTURING

introduces a new sticky tape to replace nails for hanging stuff on your walls.

Working out of his basement, **RICHARD R. WALTON** of Boston invents a shrink-proofing treatment for undershirts.

Du Pont is manufacturing a disposable toothbrush with built-in toothpaste which is being distributed through J.L. Watkins Co. of Havelock, North Carolina.

WET *no more*

The Diaper Cry is a gadget made of moisture-sensitive rubber wired to a small battery-powered speaker, which is hung on the crib. A rubber patch is placed on the baby and when the diaper is wet, mom is alerted and comes running in with a dry diapie.

$1 BILLION DOWN THE DRAIN FROM BAD CHECKS

Telecredit, Inc., of Los Angeles has developed a system for quickly verifying checks via telephone, which will cut down on the number of bad checks that are passed off each year.

A Quicker, Easier Way To Lose Your Money

The world's first electronic betting system has been developed by Electronic Assistance Corp. of New Jersey.

ADDING ON THE RUN

National Cash Register Company has invented a battery-powered, portable adding machine which delivers enough energy for an average day's work.

Catching Those SUNBEAMS

Two Illinois scientists have developed an air-conditioning system that runs on solar energy.

Using the jet engine as a model, **Jet-Heet, Inc. of Englewood, N.J.** has developed a **3-in-1 system** for the home, which includes heating, air-conditioning and hot water.

PASSINGS

Dead at age 66, in 1948 Giovanni Achille Gaggia invented a spring-powered piston that revolutionized espresso machines and forever improved the taste of coffee.

Creator, accidentally, of Crepes Suzette, Henri Charpentier dies at age 81.

WHAT A YEAR IT WAS!

SCIENCE

1962

Telstar

COMMUNICATIONS SATELLITE

AWARDS:

MARGUERITE PEREY is the first woman admitted to the French Academy of Sciences in its 200-year history for her discovery of the chemical element actinium K in 1939.

DR. RICHARD P. FEYNMAN, a professor of theoretical physics at Caltech, is one of the recipients of the Ernest O. Lawrence Memorial Award of $5,000 from the Atomic Energy Commission for his contribution in developing atomic energy.

DR. EDWARD TELLER receives the Enrico Fermi Award from the Atomic Energy Commission for his contribution to chemical and nuclear physics.

The European Space Research Organization is established in Paris with French physicist **PIERRE V. AUGER** as its first general director.

In conjunction with NASA, Bell Telephone Laboratories launches **Telstar**, a 170-pound satellite used to relay television programs from the U.S. to Europe and vice versa as well as other types of communication.

A New York newspaper sends 5,000 words to Paris at a rate 16 ½ times faster than radio or cable using the **Telstar** communications satellite.

A COMPUTER!

To help with their homework, engineering students at Case Institute of Technology are being supplied with experimental portable analog computers the size of six cigarette packs that can integrate, add, subtract and multiply.

Astronaut John H. Glenn, Jr. is a national hero when he becomes the first American to orbit the earth.

This is a year of spectacular space achievements.

The climax of three years of effort, his flight will spur new efforts to beat the Russians to the moon.

It is a down to earth welcome for the astronaut as he is greeted by his wife and Vice President Lyndon B. Johnson. There are tears of supreme happiness.

A cheering nation heaps honors on Glenn, whose 80,000-mile odyssey helps the United States blaze a trail to the stars.

WHAT A YEAR IT WAS!

BIT THE EARTH — 1962

The U.S. pushes its space program still further ahead when Scott Carpenter follows in Glenn's star-studded footsteps.

Scott brings back more data that scientists term "invaluable."

Uncle Sam's most ambitious space flight follows quickly as Commander Walter M. Schirra makes six orbits of the earth. So great is his success that the United States is now prepared to move more quickly into the larger "Gemini" program, a two-man capsule and the "Apollo" moon craft.

The commander and his family visit with President Kennedy at the White House. Schirra, along with John Glenn and Scott Carpenter, will be recorded in the history books as pioneers of 1962.

1962

A laser is bounced off the surface of the moon by MIT engineers in 2 1/2 seconds.

U.S. rocket RANGER IV crashes on the dark side of moon traveling 231,486 miles at a speed of 5,400 mph in 64 hours.

The Soviets launch rocket to Mars.

U.S. rocket RANGER III strays off path, misses moon by over 20,000 miles.

COSMOS IV is returned to earth after more than 72 hours in space.

Russians launch COSMOS III.

Reentering earth after completing the second American manned orbital flight in his spacecraft AURORA VII, Scott Carpenter misses the designated landing point in the Caribbean due to a three-second delay of retrofire which causes the craft to overshoot splashdown by around 250 miles. The Navy finds him after searching for 39 minutes and he is rescued.

The U.S.'s MARINER II spacecraft gives mankind its first close-up observations of Venus.

At Montana's Malmstrom Air Force Base, the first 20 MINUTEMAN missiles become operational.

Russians launch COSMOS IV.

The U.S. Air Force unveils a jet-pack that allows an astronaut to leave his spaceship to make repairs or visit a friend on another spaceship.

An **electrothermal rocket** to propel space vehicles is patented by the National Aeronautics and Space Administration.

Nine new astronauts are selected:

Neil Armstrong	Elliot See
Frank Borman	Thomas Stafford
Charles Conrad, Jr.	Edward White
James Lovell	John Young
James McDivitt	

The Soviets set another space first by sending twin manned spacecraft into nearly identical orbits with the first spacecraft VOSTOK III, piloted by **ANDRIAN NIKOLAYEV**, orbiting the earth a record 64 times. VOSTOK IV, piloted by **PAVEL POPOVICH**, follows two days later with the second pilot orbiting 48 times in 70 hours and 57 minutes.

The U.S.S. THOMAS A. EDISON is the U.S. Navy's eighth nuclear-powered POLARIS submarine to join the fleet at Groton, Connecticut.

A leading British scientist tells us that the internal temperature of the moon may be 1000 to 2000C.

An Air Force AEROBEE rocket is launched housing the first X-ray detector used in astronomy.

U.S. and Russian scientists agree on a world weather watch which calls for increasing the number of observation centers, collecting, analyzing and disseminating weather information and cooperation in launching weather satellites.

An orbiting solar observatory is launched out of Cape Canaveral to study an 11-year cycle of sunspot activity.

Using echo sounding, the British Navy reports a record oceanic depth of 37,782 feet in the Mindanao trench east of the Philippines.

In the bathyscape *Archimede*, French explorers **Georges Huot** and **Pierre Henri Willm** dive over 30,365 feet into the Pacific Ocean and search the Japan Trench bottom for three hours.

In a joint project between Britain and the U.S., the first international satellite is fired into orbit from Cape Canaveral.

Explorer 16, the first satellite for meteorite studies only, is launched out of Cape Canaveral.

IS ANYBODY OUT THERE?

Some of the world's top biologists, paleontologists, physicists and chemists gather at the New York Academy of Sciences to discuss the latest evidence on extraterrestrial life.

The *U.S.S. Seadragon* moors at the North Pole after its historic meeting under the polar ice with the *U.S.S. Skate*.

As a result of a frozen channel discovered under the 1,200-mile long Antarctica Peninsula, scientists conclude that what was thought to be the world's longest peninsula may be an island.

1962

THE U.S. PUBLIC HEALTH SERVICE

finds the levels of radioactive iodine 131 fallout exceeds peacetime protective standards in milk despite U.S. and Soviet atomic testing.

Dr. Benjamin Spock, child-care expert, becomes a peace activist, joins SANE (National Committee for a Sane Nuclear Policy) and takes out a full-page ad in THE NEW YORK TIMES expressing his fear for our future.

atomic particles

Physicists at the Brookhaven National Laboratory find that the most elusive of atomic particles, the neutrino, has neither mass nor electric charge and can, therefore, pass through materials such as steel with the ease of a rocket through space.

energy

● In a report sent to the President, the **Atomic Energy Commission** concludes that atomic energy is almost as economical a fuel as oil, gas and coal in high power-cost areas such as California and New England.

● New York City's **Consolidated Edison** announces plans to build the nation's largest atomic power plant.

● In order to generate more power, **Pacific Gas & Electric** begins construction on a second plant in Northern California to tap into natural steam geysers.

● Atomic energy marks the 20th anniversary of its birth with ceremonies held at the University of Chicago.

● Concern over recently formed radiation belt causes U.S. to revise its nuclear test schedule.

● The U.S. has 200 atomic reactors in operation while Britain and Russia each have 39.

● Engineers at the University of Florida develop an air-conditioning unit that uses solar energy to cool things off.

Research centers in Europe and America simultaneously discover the Anti-Xi-Minus antiparticles.

Teams of researchers at Johns Hopkins and Northwestern universities discover another atomic particle – The Eta Meson.

NORMAN F. RAMSEY, DANIEL KLEPPNER and **H. MARK GOLDENBERG** of Harvard University develop an atomic clock that will gain or lose only a few seconds in 100,000 years.

WHAT A YEAR IT WAS!

A U.S. submarine detonates a **POLARIS** missile near Christmas Island in the Pacific in the first launching of a long-range nuclear missile.

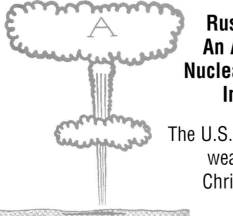

Russia Sets Off An Atmospheric Nuclear Explosion In The Arctic.

The U.S. ends nuclear weapons tests at Christmas Island.

The U.S. sets off a thermonuclear explosion 250 miles above Johnson Island in the Pacific which creates spectacular auroral displays visible in the night sky from Hawaii to New Zealand.

As part of the AEC program to use nuclear explosions for peaceful purposes, the largest nuclear explosion in U.S. history is set off 650 feet underground at Nevada's Yucca Flat.

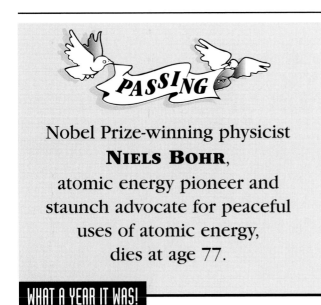

PASSING

Nobel Prize-winning physicist **NIELS BOHR**, atomic energy pioneer and staunch advocate for peaceful uses of atomic energy, dies at age 77.

British biologists report that a hormonal reaction in the insect's brain is responsible for causing locusts to swarm together with each one eating more than its own weight daily.

Rachel Carson's best seller Silent Spring alerts the nation to the dangers of using pesticides.

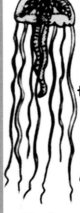

French deep sea explorer Jacques-Yves Cousteau predicts that in 50 years there will be another race of men called HOMO AQUATICUS, or the Water Man, who will be born, live and die entirely beneath the sea.

Molten magma continuously renews the ocean floors by flowing up through rifts then spreading them out laterally according to a theory presented in the paper "History of Ocean Basins."

Russian scientist Chudinov revives fossil algae thought to be 250 million-years-old.

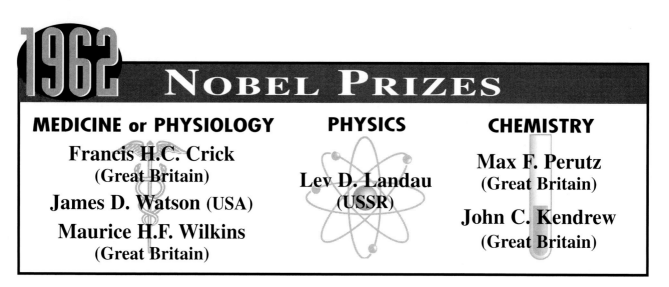

MEDICINE or PHYSIOLOGY
Francis H.C. Crick
(Great Britain)
James D. Watson (USA)
Maurice H.F. Wilkins
(Great Britain)

PHYSICS
Lev D. Landau
(USSR)

CHEMISTRY
Max F. Perutz
(Great Britain)

John C. Kendrew
(Great Britain)

With the discovery of tiny fossils in ancient sedimentary rock on the north shore of Lake Superior, the history of animal life on earth is pushed back another 1,500,000 years according to Harvard University biologist Elso S. Barghoorn.

Nobel Prize winner **Dr. Francis H.C. Crick** of Cambridge University excites the scientific community with his experiments designed to crack the genetic code by suggesting that the four chemical bases of RNA always arrange themselves by threes. With a letter standing for each of the four bases, 64 three-letter "words" would be possible with the trick being to find the 20 words that represent each of the 20 amino acids, the building blocks of protein.

THEM BONES, THEM BONES, THEM TRUNK BONES

Enormous bones of an extinct species of elephant, along with hundreds of stone tools, are discovered in Spain designating it the earliest known residence of Stone Age man in Europe, approximately 300,000 - 400,000 years ago.

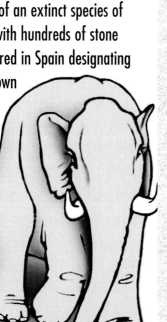

Huge color paintings of animals, birds and Indians wearing head-dresses are discovered in a remote cave in Baja, California and according to A UCLA Professor, are among the best ever found on the American continent.

The Mayans of Central America's system of writing, the only original written language developed in the Western Hemisphere, is deciphered by three Soviet mathematicians using a computer to interpret the hieroglyphics.

Medicine

THERE MAY NOT BE A DOCTOR IN THE HOUSE

With only 60,000 general practitioners in the country and less medical students wanting the pressures of that kind of practice, the family doctor is becoming a vanishing breed.

A Harvard University doctor challenges the state of health care in America saying that at least a dozen countries have a lower infant mortality rate, and that in the U.S. average life expectancy is 66 vs. 75 in Sweden and 74 in England. Dr. Osler L. Peterson also says that if the Federal Government pays the doctor bills, there will not be a decline in the nation's health care.

ANY OTHER IMPROVEMENTS IN INCHES??

Men are growing taller and getting wider, according to insurance companies, with men averaging an inch more in height than their dads bringing them to 5' 10" and around 25 pounds heavier than their grandfathers.

ARE YOU GETTING FLAKY ON ME?

In experiments being conducted at Chicago Medical School, people suffering from dandruff have gotten relief with a drug called biphenamine hydrochloride, which is mixed into an experimental shampoo.

The JOURNAL OF THE AMERICAN MEDICAL ASSOCIATION reports on a new test that can measure whether a pain is real or psychosomatic based on the patient's psycho-galvanic reflex.

IS THERE A DOCTOR IN THE HOUSE WHO SPEAKS ENGLISH?

The American Medical Association says that 11,000 new doctors will be needed within the next ten years and to meet this demand the U.S. will have to take 750 to 800 graduates of foreign medical schools a year.

RUN FOR THE HILLS—IT'S THAT TIME OF THE MONTH AGAIN

The female sex hormone estradiol can effect the body's central nervous system causing monthly swings in feminine temperament and can possibly account for a woman's generally more excitable nature, according to physiologists at the University of California at Berkeley.

AND THEY'RE MURDER TO SLEEP ON

Brush rollers worn to bed by a lot of women seem to be responsible for patches of hair loss.

Redheads are hypersensitive to pain and require more anesthesia for the same procedure than their blond or brunette counterparts.

CRUTCHES AWAY!! Thanks to the Salk vaccine, polio is no longer a significant health problem.

1962

ARF ARF—*ACHOO*

Researchers at the Northwestern University Medical School find that dogs suffer from the same allergy symptoms during ragweed seasons as people including red eyes, hay fever and asthma.

SOMETHING TO CLUCK ABOUT

Scientists from the University of Chicago tell us that chickens, and hens in particular, appear to have a higher resistance to atomic fallout than mammals and suggest that you raise chickens in your backyard if your neighbors don't object.

THERE WASN'T AN UNHAPPY PEEP OUT OF THEM

The aging process is slowed down in baby chicks fed food high in amino acids.

MONKEY SEE MONKEY MONKEY LIKE MONKEY

Monkeys watching movies at the University of Chicago seem to enjoy films about other monkeys but are less attentive when snakes appear on the screen.

WHAT DID YOU SAY?

According to the Public Health Service, with U.S. cities becoming noisier, around one out of every 15 people is suffering a hearing loss.

FOR PETE'S SAKE, WOULD YOU TURN UP THAT AWFUL MUSIC!

Research conducted at Duke University's Center for the Study of Aging reveals that as people age, they need more light and the sound turned up vs. when they are young and seek quiet and soft lighting.

BUT MOM, THE DOCTOR SAID I HAVE TO WATCH TV

Contrary to the old wives' tales that holding reading material too close to the eyes or reading in the dark or lying down harms the eyes, the more you use them, the healthier they stay according to Dr. Morris Kaplan, University of Colorado ophthalmologist. He also urges his patients to watch television as much as possible to keep the eyes normal and healthy.

As in other industrialized nations,

in the U.S.S.R. heart disease ranks first and cancer second as the most popular cause of death.

JUST A HEARTBEAT AWAY

A new technique called radiotelemetry allows doctors to monitor the heart rate of patients while they are sleeping.

Household chores are more taxing on heart attack patients then going back to work.

CLOG THE ARTERIES *FOG THE BRAIN*

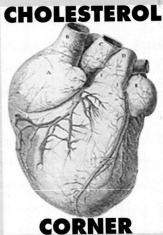

CHOLESTEROL
CORNER

Studies conducted at the Indiana University School of Medicine on healthy men between the ages of 25 to 65 indicate that those with lower cholesterol levels exhibit greater mental sharpness.

Contrary to the currently held belief, the body does not reduce its manufacturing of cholesterol to compensate for a high-cholesterol diet.

HOW TO CONTROL HARDENING OF THE ARTERIES:

- Keep your weight down
- Control high blood pressure
- Stay in treatment for other diseases such as diabetes or kidney disorders
- Eat a low-fat diet
- Use drugs to block absorption of cholesterol

- Using a donor from outside the family, the first human kidney transplant is performed.
- The severed arm of 12-year-old Everett Knowles, Jr. is successfully reattached after he loses it in a train accident.
- The first use of a laser in eye surgery is used at New York's Columbia-Presbyterian Medical Center.
- The Veterans Administration Hospital in Indianapolis performs the first brain operation using hypnosis in conjunction with anesthesia.

The American Cancer Society predicts that approximately 173,000 people will be saved from cancer this year through early detection.

Grants from the U.S. Public Health Service make possible the establishment of a $3,300,000 medical computer center at UCLA Medical School.

IT MAY SOUND CORNY, BUT…

Members of the American Podiatry Association gather in Washington to celebrate its 50th anniversary.

THEY'RE IN A BLOODY MESS NOW

Federal authorities step in and stop Westchester Blood Service, Inc. which has been changing the expiration date on blood and selling the worthless blood to hospitals.

Claiming that the new health plan will give the government total control over their profession, 700 doctors in the Canadian province of Saskatchewan go on strike.

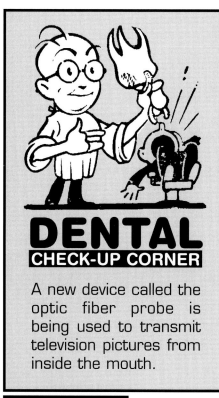

DENTAL
CHECK-UP CORNER

A new device called the optic fiber probe is being used to transmit television pictures from inside the mouth.

SMILELESS & TOOTHLESS IN THE U.S.

NUMBER OF AMERICANS

No Teeth	21,000,000
Tooth Decay	97,000,000
Periodontal Disease	23,000,000
Oral Cancer	23,000

With the growing shortage of dentists in America, the American Dental Association is calling for more women to join therapeutic teams and says that patients of tomorrow will be seeing more and more women cleaning teeth.

A SPIT'S THROW FROM TOOTH DECAY

The New York University Dental Center finds that certain people have saliva that protects them from tooth decay.

1962
All In The Mind

The National Institute of Health spends nearly $10 million in research on schizophrenia, the most widespread mental disease requiring hospitalization.

Emotional stress such as anger, fear or depression appears to increase fatty acids in the bloodstream.

Around one-fourth of people entering mental institutions do so at their own request.

Russian professor G. Yu. Malis has a theory that schizophrenia may be caused by a virus and writes about it in his book entitled *Research on the Etiology of Schizophrenia*, which is translated into English.

Psychiatric researchers at Washington University discover that schizophrenic patients have a peculiar odor after testing their perspiration, blood and urine.

DO DO THAT VOODOO THAT YOU DO SO WELL

Citing cases of voodoo deaths, an article appearing in the *Journal of the American Medical Association* indicates that a patient's psychological make-up will strongly influence how he is effected and recovers from disease.

In an article appearing in *Mental Hygiene*, Dr. Alex Kaplan writes that Russian mental institutions seem to be better staffed than those in the U.S., and the treatment is more interactive with the patients and may include massage, work assignments, medication and sports activities.

Volunteers in an experiment measuring the reaction to violence become very aggressive after watching a filmed knife fight and are willing to inflict pain. In contrast, another group who watches an educational film does not display any violent impulses.

According to a University of Chicago psychiatrist, moving old people from one institution to another appears to shorten their life spans.

Mental stress appears to be linked to the body, producing a thyroid gland substance called thyroid autoantibodies

I DON'T WANT TO TELL TALES, BUT DID YOU HEAR ABOUT MARGARET'S HUSBAND AND THE SECRETARY?

Psychiatrist Fred Feldman of Beverly Hills and the University of Southern California concludes that gossip, unless excessive or vindictive, is actually good for your mental health as a valuable release from inner tensions.

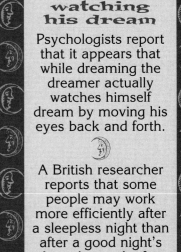

watching the dreamer dreaming watching his dream

Psychologists report that it appears that while dreaming the dreamer actually watches himself dream by moving his eyes back and forth.

A British researcher reports that some people may work more efficiently after a sleepless night than after a good night's sleep due to the fact that the mind is more aroused with sleep deprivation.

Patients treated at the Medical Clinic of the Massachusetts General Hospital for physical complaints such as fatigue are often suffering from depression.

JUST WHISTLE A HAPPY TUNE

Researchers at Johns Hopkins University School of Medicine find that happy people recover faster from the flu than their sad or depressed counterparts.

THE MIDTOWN MANHATTAN STUDY
EFFECTS OF LIFE IN THE BIG CITY
(Cornell University Medical School 10-year Study Of 175,000 People Living In New York City)

81% Emotionally Disturbed

23% Serious Neuroses

58% Milder Neuroses

Mental Illness:

Jews	**17%**
Catholics	**26%**
Protestants	**22%**

Income More Than $6,000 Yearly
(top economic group)
Only one in eight have
severe emotional problems

Income Less Than $2,800 Yearly
(lowest economic group)
Almost half are mentally disturbed

AMERICA'S SOCIAL PROBLEMS

- **Family breakdown**
- **Illegitimate births**
- **Divorce rate** *(one in four marriages ends in divorce)*
- **Juvenile delinquency**
- **Increased mental problems**

The average college freshman starts college by restraining his impulses by being morally strict with himself and others in a search for perfectionism and moral heroes and is disillusioned when he discovers that even his heroes have some human weaknesses.

With academic standards geared to the "average" child in American schools, chairman of the Psychiatry Department at New York Medical College charges that schools may be producing neurotic children when mental handicaps are not taken into consideration with regard to their learning abilities.

FAR OUT MAN, HE'S GIVING US DRUGS FOR FREE

Much to the chagrin of his associates, Harvard Professor **Timothy Leary** enlists almost all of Harvard's Psychology Department's 32 graduate students to assist him in his LSD research.

STANDING IN THE VORTEX OF A RAINBOW-COLORED FART

In response to the psychiatric community's concern about the possible misuse of LSD, the U.S. Food and Drug Administration exerts control over all projects involving this volatile, experimental drug.

A STICKY SITUATION

Teenagers across the country participate in the newest fad called glue sniffing resulting in violent behavior, kidney damage and addiction.

1962

HEY CAN YOU MAKE ME A KID WHO CAN HIT A HOME RUN WITH THE BASES LOADED AT THE TOP OF THE 9TH?

Within two generations human sperm banks will be used to improve the genetic fitness of children according to Nobel Prize-winning geneticist, Hermann J. Muller.

MAKE VUN MOOF AND I'LL PRESS THE BUTTON

Dr. Otto Schmitt, head of the Department of Biophysics at the University of Minnesota, says science can exercise technological control over human behavior through the use of radio-controlled pellets of medication implanted in the body which can stimulate or depress certain kinds of behaviors.

FINGERPRINTS TODAY VOICEPRINTS TOMORROW

Acoustics researcher at Bell Telephone Laboratories, Lawrence G. Kersta, predicts that someday your voice may serve as a means of identification as accurate as your fingerprints because of the uniqueness of the voice.

After studying the correlation between respiratory infection and the content of sulfur particles in the atmosphere, Dr. F.C. Donhan of the University of Pennsylvania concludes that there is a link to air pollution and the common cold.

Lowering the age from 65, the Public Health Service now recommends that anyone over 45 should have a flu shot.

SMILE, YOU'RE ON CAMERA

Dr. Russell H. Morgan, Director of Radiology at Johns Hopkins Hospital, develops a system whereby moving images of X-ray examinations can be recorded on magnetic tape via a television tape recorder which can be played back instantly allowing the doctor to evaluate the patient.

NEXT HE'LL TELL US HIGH FAT DIETS ARE A MUST

Dr. Gordon C. Ring of the Center for Study of Cellular Aging at the University of Miami says that there is no evidence that exercising will prolong one's life span and asserts that the opposite is true.

Citing that well-meaning visitors can actually hurt patients, Dr. Claude L. Brown of Mobile, Alabama urges hospitals to set up visiting hours and to limit the number of visitors per patient during those designated hours.

OKAY, LIE DOWN AND SAY BRRRRRR

Doctors at the University of Minnesota are healing ulcers through the application of ice on patients' stomachs.

HOW TO DEVELOP AN ULCER IN 10 EASY WAYS

1. Make your job #1 priority at the expense of your family.
2. Never play as it's a waste of time.
3. Always carry your briefcase so you can work anywhere.
4. Take on more jobs than you can handle.
5. Never delegate. Do everything yourself.
6. Crack the whip on your subordinates.
7. Schedule out-of-town appointments so that you work all day and travel all night to get to the next one.
8. Take lots of Benzedrine.
9. Snort a quick drink before a meeting to clear your mind and a few martinis before dinner.
10. Eat only when hungry and ignore your doctor's advice on diet.

SMOKE NOW, PAY LATER

The British Government begins a nonsmoking campaign including posters and banning cigarette advertising before 9:00 p.m. due to a report issued by the Royal College of Physicians connecting smoking to lung cancer.

THE BEST THINGS IN LIFE AREN'T ALWAYS FREE

In a strongly-worded message, the Air Force Surgeon General's office issues a directive banning giving out cigarettes provided free by tobacco companies to patients in its military hospitals due to increasing evidence linking cigarette smoking to lung cancer.

- Chronic cigarette cough is a reality according to a 10-year study conducted in Philadelphia among men over 45.

- An article appearing in the A.M.A. *Journal* reports that filter tip cigarettes may reduce the risk of lung cancer.

If alcohol consumed during the cocktail hour is in moderation, the results can be pleasant, with the banal conversations, lousy canapes and dopey jokes all taking on a most enjoyable tone.

Alcoholism among women is extremely high and hard to detect with at least 2 1/2 million women out of the estimated five million Americans with this disease.

IT MAKES ME ITCHY THINKING ABOUT IT

The National Institute of Health announces that the virus causing German measles has been isolated and that a vaccine can now be developed.

The World Forum on Syphilis and the International Congress of Dermatology report that there is a large upsurge in the number of syphilis cases documented from around the world, with the U.S. stating 9,000,000 Americans were formerly or are presently infected with a disease that was thought to be under control.

OH MY ACHING BACK

If you've got an aching back chances are someone in your family had one too, as back problems such as slipped discs are hereditary, according to Dr. Benjamin R. Wiltberger of Ohio State University.

PUTTING THE BONES OUT   TO DRY

Contrary to popular belief, living in a warmer, dryer climate is not a cure for arthritis according to the Arthritis and Rheumatism Foundation.

The Harvard Medical School announces the development of a new test than can reveal cancer of the kidney before clinical symptoms manifest.

In a test, 55% to 60% of patients suffering from arthritis feel relief after taking a placebo.

1962

A report appearing in the **Journal of Pediatrics** indicates that it does not appear to make any difference whether you give your baby cold or warm formula. It seems to be all the same to the baby.

Washington reports that premature births are linked to smoking in pregnancy.

The 174th General Assembly of the United Presbyterian Church upholds the right of married couples to practice birth control, artificial insemination and sex education for young people.

THE SOUND OF TWO HEARTS BEATING

Ultrasound is being used at New York's Columbia-Presbyterian Hospital to determine if there is more than one fetus.

IS THERE A HOOVER IN THE HOUSE?

Russia begins performing vacuum abortions for pregnancies.

SHOO WOP, SHOO WOP, DOO, DOO, SHOO WOP, SHOO WOP, DOO, DOO

Transmitting sounds through the expectant mother's abdominal wall, obstetricians at London's University College Hospital discover babies in the womb can hear musical sounds and respond with an accelerated heartbeat.

PASSING
Creator of the *Pap smear* which helps detect uterine cancer, **Dr. George Papanicolaou** dies at age 78.

Thousands of deformed babies are born in Europe as a result of mothers taking a sleeping aid called thalidomide. **Dr. Frances O. Kelsey**, of the U.S. Food and Drug Administration, averts similar American tragedies by preventing the drug from being sold in the U.S. for which she receives the President's Award for Distinguished Service from **President Kennedy**, who cites her great courage and devotion to the public interest.

As a result of the thalidomide tragedy, Congress passes the Drug Amendments Act of 1962 with some of the following provisions:

- Drugs must be proven safe and effective.
- The name of the drug as well as the generic name must be on the label.
- Every batch of antibiotic drugs must be government inspected.
- Every drug factory must be registered.
- All advertising of the medical industry must include possible side effects.
- FDA can seize products from pharmaceutical manufacturers who don't follow good manufacturing procedures.

146

WHAT A YEAR IT WAS!

YUM! MYSTERY MEAT, MASHED POTATOES & VANILLA TAPIOCA

A recent poll by the National Opinion Research Center of 1,000 patients in 50 Massachusetts hospitals reveals that most patients are satisfied with hospital food.

WHAT DO YOU MEAN PASS THE SUGAR, GET IT YOURSELF

Americans are consuming over 100 billion cups of coffee a year which is causing some negative side effects such as irritability and withdrawal symptoms including headache and fatigue.

DON'T HAVE ONE FOR THE ROAD

Indiana University Medical Center scientists discover that the caffeine in the last cup of coffee a person has before driving can have the same effect as alcohol by impairing the driver's decision-making capabilities.

Useless food supplements promising good health are costing ten million Americans over $500 million a year.

FEAR OF FATTENING

Lipophobes are petite women with delicate features and slight frames whose fear of getting fat sends them to see physicians to find ways of getting thinner either through stricter diets or medication.

LOSE A POUND— HAVE A LAUGH

Dieting does not appear to produce depression and as the dieter sees results they actually feel less anxious.

WELL I GUESS ICE CREAM AND POTATO CHIPS FOR DESSERT ARE OUT OF THE QUESTION

America is on a protein binge with fat being ignored because of concern over heart attacks and carbohydrates being shunned by people on diets.

NO MORE ROLLER NIGHTMARES ... (ever!)

Found! a carefree new concept in hair care!

sho-curl® 7-day hair setting lotion
* * * * * * * * * *

The Lotion Discovery that brings you Once-a-Week Hair Control—Now you can keep your hairdo for 7 days!

Let Sho-Curl show you the once-a-week way to beautiful hair. It's a breeze!

Just shampoo your hair as usual. (You'll wash away all your old ideas about hair care forever.) Then set your hair in your favorite way with Sho-Curl 7-Day Hair Setting Lotion.

That's all!

From day-to-day, for a whole wonderful week, a comb is all you need. Sho-Curl sets quickly, dries quickly, adds the beautiful body that makes your hair style last longer. Sound like a dream? Try Sho-Curl and see! Be a sleeping beauty every night—while your hair looks its loveliest all week!

Another discovery for lovelier hair from Formula 42...makers of Sho-Curl Hair Spray for normal and hard-to-hold hair—Lemonized Creme Shampoo, Mint Creme Shampoo, Lathering Oil Shampoo.

sho-curl®
7 DAY
HAIR SETTING LOTION
SETS QUICKLY ★ ADDS BODY

This professional secret is now yours from Formula 42

Discover the remarkable principle of hair control, used successfully for five years by professional hairdressers. Now Formula 42 brings you the secret of the salons—with amazing Sho-Curl. Why not start your first week's vacation from rollers today!

®1962 42 Products Ltd., Inc.

Special Introductory Offer **99¢**

plus Fed. Tax

WHEREVER FINE TOILETRIES ARE SOLD

148

Do The Math

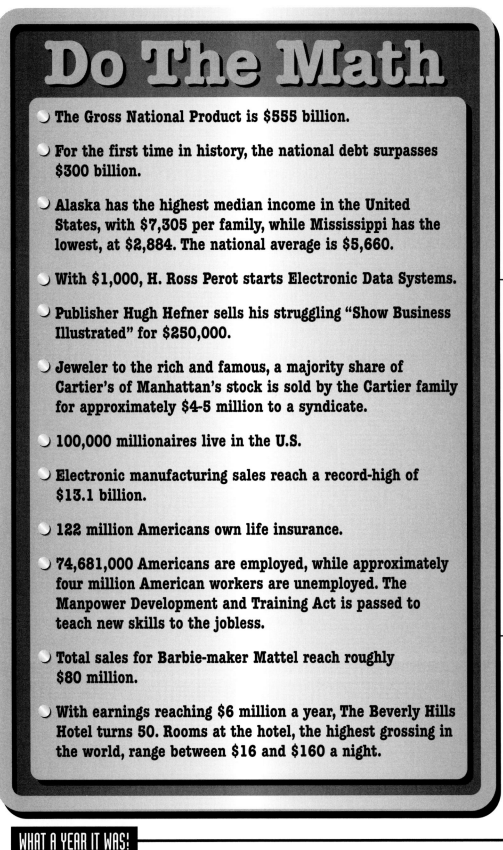

- The Gross National Product is $555 billion.

- For the first time in history, the national debt surpasses $300 billion.

- Alaska has the highest median income in the United States, with $7,305 per family, while Mississippi has the lowest, at $2,884. The national average is $5,660.

- With $1,000, H. Ross Perot starts Electronic Data Systems.

- Publisher Hugh Hefner sells his struggling "Show Business Illustrated" for $250,000.

- Jeweler to the rich and famous, a majority share of Cartier's of Manhattan's stock is sold by the Cartier family for approximately $4-5 million to a syndicate.

- 100,000 millionaires live in the U.S.

- Electronic manufacturing sales reach a record-high of $13.1 billion.

- 122 million Americans own life insurance.

- 74,681,000 Americans are employed, while approximately four million American workers are unemployed. The Manpower Development and Training Act is passed to teach new skills to the jobless.

- Total sales for Barbie-maker Mattel reach roughly $80 million.

- With earnings reaching $6 million a year, The Beverly Hills Hotel turns 50. Rooms at the hotel, the highest grossing in the world, range between $16 and $160 a night.

The **"Shopmobile"** brings the general store to the neighborhood as a large bus filled with merchandise roams around Orlando, Florida.

Approximately 375 billion trading stamps are issued this year, and are traded in for toasters and other household items. Major companies include **S&H Green Stamps**, **Blue Chip** and **King Korn**.

 The typical American employee earns double their European counterpart.

1962

Paper currency in the United States celebrates its 100th birthday.

Yogi Berra *becomes vice president of* **YOO-HOO** *Chocolate Beverage Company.*

ROAD SHOW

🚗 Foreign-made automobiles account for just under 5% of all cars sold in America.

🚗 Americans purchase almost 200,000 Volkswagen Beetles.

🚗 6,750,000 American-made cars are sold, with approximately one million being Chevrolets.

🚗 About one in two new cars on U.S. roads is made by General Motors.

🚗 Ford begins work on the country's first "compact compact," smaller than your average compact car.

The U.S. Bureau of Labor Statistics calculates that several hundred thousand workers will lose their jobs to automation over the next ten years.

The future of downtown American shopping districts is revealed when Midtown Plaza opens in Rochester, New York. The $30 million enclosed shopping center boasts plentiful parking which gets shoppers out of their cars and into the stores.

5,000 people attend the United States Savings and Loan League's 70th yearly convention.

COFFEE, TEA OR CLAIROL

Stewardesses of major airlines hold a press conference to protest the airlines' rule that their hair color must be mousy brown.

The Civil Aeronautics Board begins fining airlines that overbook flights and passengers who fail to show up for their flights.

Hughes Tool Co. is given permission by the Civil Aeronautics Board to purchase a controlling interest of Northeast Airlines.

Sam Walton opens the first **Wal-Mart** in Rogers, Arkansas.

•

The first **Kmart** store opens in Garden City, Michigan.

•

Holiday Inn opens its 200th hotel (in Palm Springs, California).

150

19 million work days are lost due to strikes.

David Dubinsky is elected to his 11th term as President of the International Ladies' Garment Workers' Union.

Several unions strike against Minneapolis' "Tribune" and "Star" for 113 days, setting a new strike record for the newspaper business.

At New York's glamorous Waldorf-Astoria Hotel, white collar workers are forced to provide services when cooks, waiters, elevator operators and bellhops strike for 2 1/2 days.

The "New York Daily News" is shut down for eight days by a strike of the New York Newspaper Guild.

6,500 United Auto Workers strike against Studebaker-Packard for 40 days in Indiana while 3,000 strike against Champion Spark Plug in Ohio for several weeks.

600 Flight Engineers International members strike against Eastern Airlines for two months, adversely effecting 18,000 employees.

The average workweek for a factory worker is 40 1/2 hours.

Members of Manhattan's International Brotherhood of Electrical Workers Local 3 win the shortest workweek in U.S. industry – 25 hours plus five hours of overtime.

FULL STEAM AHEAD

1,000 Order of Railroad Telegraphers strike for one month against the Chicago & North Western Railway, shutting down the company's operations.

The big railroads come to a wage increase agreement with 450,000 workers.

*With **President Kennedy's** intervention, a steel strike is averted and a new "noninflationary" contract is signed, effecting all U.S. steel workers. Shortly thereafter, U.S. Steel and smaller steel companies raise their prices $6 a ton, but due to pressure from an angry president, the possibility of being investigated by the Department of Justice for antitrust practices and the loss of the Defense Department as a customer, the price hike is revoked.*

President Kennedy *invokes the Taft-Hartley Act four times. The incidents:*

1. *International Association of Machinists against Lockheed Aircraft.*
2. *9,000 employees against Republic Aviation.*
3. *12,000 members of the Seafarers International Union on the West Coast.*
4. *90,000 Longshoremen on the Gulf and Atlantic coasts.*

YEARLY WAGES

National Average:

Elementary School Graduate .	$ 3,450
High School Graduate	5,050
College Graduate	7,260
Bookkeeper	$ 6,500
Controller	15,000
Copywriter	7,800
Draftsman	8,000
Editor	8,200
Electrical Engineer	12,000
Executive Secretary	7,000
Home Economist	8,000
Insurance Claim Adjuster	5,200
Lucille Ball, VP, Desilu Productions	25,000
Market Analyst	10,000
Military Personnel	3,800
Radio Program Director	12,000
Sales Analyst	7,500
Teacher	5,300

IT'S THE LAW

In a case that began in 1955, the Supreme Court bars **Kinney Shoes** from merging with **Brown Shoe Company**.

A federal judge in Chicago orders **E.I. du Pont de Nemours & Co.** to divest itself of $3.5 billion of **General Motors** stock by 1965.

General Electric agrees to pay the government $7,470,000 for price-fixing.

PASSINGS

E.F. Hutton Co. founder and ardent believer in democracy which led him to start the Freedoms Foundation Inc., **Edward Francis Hutton** dies at age 85.

Former president and current chairman of the board of Maytag, **Frederick Louis Maytag II**, grandson of the firm's founder, dies at age 51.

WHAT A YEAR IT WAS!

STOCK MARKET NEWS

NYSE Shares traded: 962,155,308

1962

STOCKS

The average NYSE stock price: $73.20

THE NEW YORK STOCK EXCHANGE

The NYSE loses nearly $20.8 billion on Blue Monday, May 28, the biggest drop since Black Tuesday, October 28, 1929.

— — —

The Standard and Poor's composite index drops to a low of 55.63

— — —

The Dow-Jones Industrial Average declines 38.82, the largest one-week drop in history.

— — —

The Dow-Jones falls to 535.76, the lowest for the year.

— — —

Foreign investors own $12 billion in U.S. stocks.

The total market value of NYSE stocks traded: $339,800,000,000	
Ampex	16 3/4
Chrysler	53 3/8
Eastman Kodak	115 7/8
Gulf Oil	34 5/8
Hershey Chocolate	189
IBM	461
Kaiser Aluminum	35
Lionel	19 1/2
Pan Am Airlines	17 1/4
RC Cola	25 1/2
Safeway	43
Sunbeam	34 1/2
Westinghouse	39 1/8
Xerox	166 1/4
Zenith	75 5/8

1962
This Is THE PRICE THAT WAS

FOOD

	$ .10
Apples (lb.)	.10
Avocados (each)	.21
Bread (loaf)	.10
Broccoli (lb.)	.69
Butter (lb.)	.05
Cabbage (lb.)	.64
Cheddar Cheese (lb.)	

SIGNORA

Blouse	$ 8.95
Dress	25.00
Gloves (wrist length)	4.98
Lipstick	1.50
Permanent	15.00
Seamless Stockings	1.75
Shoes	12.99
Suit	25.98
Sunglasses	2.98
Wig (synthetic)	49.50
Wool Sweater	13.98

Chocolate Malt	
Coffee (lb.)	$ .20
Cucumber (each)	.59
Donut	.10
Eggs (dozen)	.07
Fruit Pie	.45
Ice Cream (1/2 gallon)	.39
Lemons (lb.)	.49
Mayonnaise (qt.)	.10
Milk (gallon)	.49
Peanuts (lb.)	.28
Pineapple (each)	.39
Rhubarb (lb.)	.29
Rice (lb.)	.19
Sugar (lb.)	.21
Tomatoes (lb.)	.11
	.19

SEÑOR

Briefs	$ 1.25
Cashmere Sweater	21.99
Dinner Jacket	42.50
Haircut	3.75
Necktie	2.19
Pajamas	5.00
Polo Shirt	7.95
Shoes	11.90
Slacks	24.50
Socks	1.50
Suit	85.00

LA CASA

Automatic Toothbrush	$ 19.75
Blender	29.95
Clock Radio	24.95
Clothes Dryer	98.88
Cookware (7 pieces)	23.88
Dishwasher	139.95
Hair Dryer	18.89
Iron	21.95
Light Bulb	.39

Phonograph	
Pillowcase	79.95
Refrigerator	1.29
Shampoo	229.95
Sheets	.63
Sofa	4.98
Teakettle	450.00
Toaster	8.95
Toothpaste	13.99
Washing Machine	.69
Waterford Crystal Goblet	176.00
	5.50

VA-ROOM

Gasoline (gallon)	$ .36
Monthly Lease:	
Cadillac	180.00
Pontiac	88.50
Muffler	5.98
Peugeot 403	2,250.00
Shock Absorbers	6.77
Tires	8.95
Triumph TR-4	2,849.00

ENTERTAINMENT

Book	$ 5.95
Bowling Ball	24.95
Broadway Show, orchestra	7.50
Concert,	
Benny Goodman in Moscow	6.66
Queen's Gallery, London	.35
Van Gogh Exhibit,	
Boston Museum of Fine Arts	1.00

Housing

3 Bedroom House:

National Average	$11,800
Memphis, Tennessee	8,675
Levittown, New York	13,390
Englewood, New Jersey	26,500
Malibu, California	35,000
New Canaan, Connecticut	39,900
Weekend Home (prefabricated)	3,599

Only twenty letters a day— and we need a postage meter?

"No, Mr. Smithers. We don't *need* a postage meter. We can still use adhesive stamps, hand-written letters, and carrier pigeons. But metered mail is faster, more businesslike, and *so* convenient. I wouldn't have to run down to the postoffice when we run out of fours or airmails. Or play a guessing game every month trying to account for postage."

Once metered mail was for big, blue chip companies. Now any lawyer, doctor, merchant or dry cleaner can use a DM— the little, low-cost desk model postage meter made for the small business.

The DM prints postage, the exact amount needed, right on the envelope; or on special tape for parcel post. With your own small ad, if you want one. Protects your postage from loss, damage, misuse. And accounts for it automatically, on registers that show postage used and on hand. Easy to use. Makes mailing faster, easier, neater. Does away with sticking stamps and moistening envelope flaps, and with pre-stamped envelopes.

Buying postage is easier. The postoffice sets your meter for the amount you want. Fewer trips to the postoffice! And metered mail is already postmarked and cancelled, needs less handling in the postoffice, can often make earlier trains and planes.

The DM costs about 30¢ a day, pays off in convenience in any office. Ask any Pitney-Bowes office for a demonstration of the DM, or any of the twelve other meter models, hand operated or powered. Or send the coupon for free booklet.

FREE: *Handy desk or wall chart of latest postal rates, with parcel post map and zone finder.*

PB Pitney-Bowes
POSTAGE METERS

Made by the leading manufacturer of mailing machines...149 offices in U.S. and Canada. In Canada: Pitney-Bowes of Canada, Ltd., Dept. 335, 909 Yonge Street, Toronto.

PITNEY-BOWES, INC.
2835 Pacific Street, Stamford, Conn.
Send free ☐ *booklet* ☐ *postal rate chart to:*

Name _____

Address _____

156

1962

DISASTERS

An earth-quake starts a snowy avalanche on Mount Huascaran, PERU which buries over a dozen villages and kills several thousand people.

Heavy fog causes an express train to crash into a commuter train in the NETHERLANDS, killing 91 and wounding approximately 200.

298 coal miners die in an explosion in Voelklingen, GERMANY.

A devastating earth-quake hits **IRAN**, killing over 12,000 people, destroying 25,000 homes and leaving more than 100,000 homeless.

In the worst single plane acci-dent in the history of aviation, an Air France Boeing 707 jet crashes just after takeoff from Paris' Orly Airport. Most of the 130 fatalities are members of the Atlanta Art Association. Two stewardesses survive the crash.

Severe flooding surrounding Barcelona, SPAIN fatally injures close to 800 and causes $80 million in damage.

In Trikkala, GREECE, 13 die and 13 are wounded when a truck falls 1,500 feet into a gorge.

70 people drown on New Year's Day when a boat sinks in INDIA'S Savithri River.

WHAT A YEAR IT WAS!

157

1962

ASIA

A Flying Tiger plane on its way to the PHILIPPINES from GUAM vanishes carrying more than 100 American and South Vietnamese soldiers.

242 people lose their lives in Sunchon, SOUTH KOREA when a flash flood breaks several dikes.

In southern THAILAND tropical storm Harriet destroys an entire village, takes the lives of nearly 800 people, injures hundreds and causes $20 million in damage.

In the U.S.

28,000 people die in home accidents while 41,000 people perish in car accidents.

Six firemen are killed in the line of duty when a fire breaks out in a MANHATTAN building.

All 95 on board perish when an American Airlines Boeing 707 crashes into Jamaica Bay, NEW YORK after takeoff from Idlewild.

An East Coast storm takes the lives of 40 people and causes $160 million in damage. Across the country in the Pacific Northwest, a storm with over 100 mph winds kills nearly 50 and brings about $150 million in damage.

SPORTS 1962

YANKEES WIN THEIR 20TH WORLD CHAMPIONSHIP

The San Francisco Giants meet the New York Yankees in the World Series.

Giants rookie Chuck Hiller makes the record book with a grand slam homer. This four-run blast is the first National League bases loaded homer in World Series history.

The fans are delighted.

It rains for days on the West Coast and for a time it looks like the only winner is the weatherman.

Another rookie, Yankee Tom Tresh, breaks up the fifth game with a three-run homer sending the teams back to San Francisco for the final tilt.

The sun finally comes out and Willie McCovey slams one to Bobby Richardson for the final out.

The Yankees win their 20th World Championship and the champs are as happy as schoolboys as they mob pitcher Ralph Terry.

WHAT A YEAR IT WAS!

1962

WORLD SERIES
New York Yankees over San Francisco Giants, 4-3

Veteran outfielder **Stan Musial** breaks Ty Cobb's major league record of 5,863 career bases when he hits a home run and two singles in a twilight doubleheader.

Dodger shortstop **Maury Wills** sets a new record of 104 stolen bases breaking Ty Cobb's mark of 96 which was unbroken since 1916.

Acting as a pinch hitter, St. Louis Cardinal **Stan Musial** singles for his 3,516th career hit placing him in second place on the all-time hit list behind Ty Cobb.

Most Valuable Player
National League
Maury Wills (LA)

American League
Mickey Mantle (NY)

Home Run Leaders
National League
Willie Mays (San Francisco, 49)

American League
Harmon Killebrew (Minnesota, 48)

Batting Champions
National League
Tommy Davis (LA, .346)

American League
Pete Runnels (Boston, .326)

Strikeouts
National League
Don Drysdale (LA, 232)

American League
Camilo Pascual (Minnesota, 206)

CY YOUNG AWARD
Don Drysdale LA

 In one of the longest games in history, the New York Yankees battle the Detroit Tigers for 22 innings with New York finally winning 9-7 after seven hours.

 At a $35,000 paycheck, **Don Drysdale** earns the highest salary ever paid to a Dodger pitcher.

Buck "John" O'Neil becomes the first black coach in Major League baseball after accepting a position with the Chicago Cubs.

The All-Star Games

National over American **3-1**

American over National **9-4**

No-Hit Games
Sandy Koufax
LA Dodgers over NY Mets, 5-0

Bo Belinsky
LA Angels over Baltimore Orioles, 2-0

The New York Mets play their first regular season game.

University of Detroit basketball star **Dave DeBusschere** signs with the Chicago White Sox as a pitcher.

The Los Angeles Dodgers start playing at Dodgers Stadium.

IMMORTALS

TYRUS RAYMOND COBB
GEORGE HERMAN RUTH
JOHN HENRY WAGNER
CHRISTOPHER MATHEWSON
WALTER P. JOHNSON
NAPOLEON LAJOIE
DENTON TECUMSEH YOUNG

BOB FELLER & JACKIE ROBINSON INDUCTED INTO THE BASEBALL HALL OF FAME

The doors of baseball's Hall of Fame have swung open to admit two more baseball immortals.

Jackie Robinson is the first black to be honored with admission to the shrine of the national game.

Pitcher Bob Feller is a one-time Iowa farm boy who became the greatest pitcher of his day.

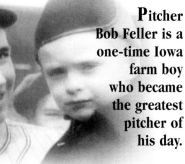

In his prime, he was baseball's most feared base runner.

He spent his entire Major League career with the Cleveland Indians.

A formidable hitter, Jackie won the National League batting crown in 1949.

In the World Series opener of 1955, he stole home against Yogi Berra and Whitey Ford.

WHAT A YEAR IT WAS!

Coupé buffet?

Food's more fun with this <u>fresh, clean taste</u>!

Want to make points *before* the game? Treat your bunch to lunch and 7-Up! Whatever you eat tastes better, brighter with sparkling 7-Up. Think how delightful with a relish-topped hot dog! Or a mustard-y ham and cheese! Seven-Up keeps your taste buds awake—so you don't miss a single flavor. Getting hungry? It's *always* 7-Up time!

FOR THIRST QUENCHING, FRESH TASTE, QUICK LIFT . . . "FRESH UP" WITH SEVEN-UP!

162

FOOTBALL 1962

NATIONAL FOOTBALL LEAGUE CHAMPIONS

Green Bay Packers over New York Giants

16-7

Vince Lombardi
Green Bay Coach

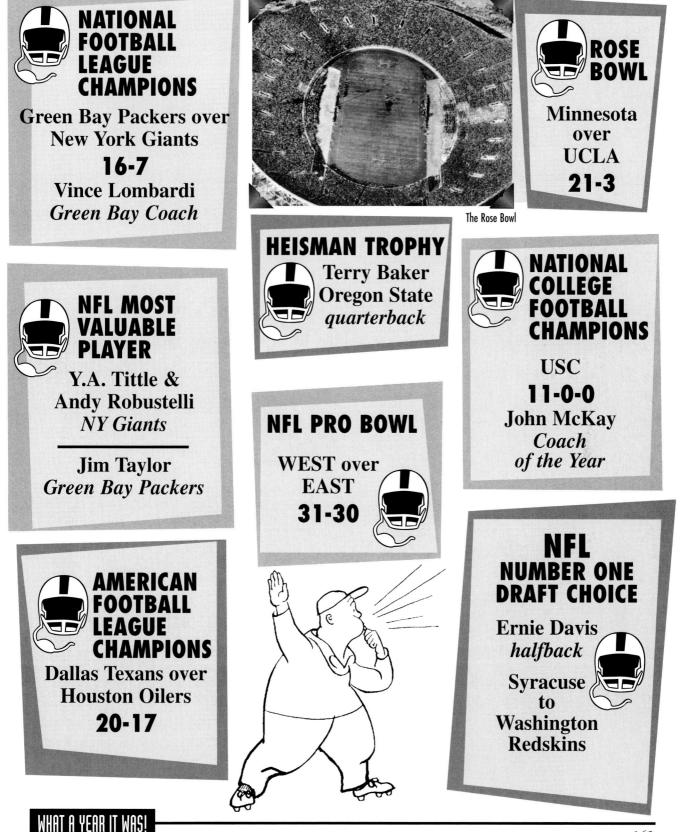

The Rose Bowl

ROSE BOWL

Minnesota over UCLA

21-3

NFL MOST VALUABLE PLAYER

Y.A. Tittle &
Andy Robustelli
NY Giants

———

Jim Taylor
Green Bay Packers

HEISMAN TROPHY

Terry Baker
Oregon State
quarterback

NATIONAL COLLEGE FOOTBALL CHAMPIONS

USC

11-0-0

John McKay
*Coach
of the Year*

NFL PRO BOWL

WEST over EAST

31-30

AMERICAN FOOTBALL LEAGUE CHAMPIONS

Dallas Texans over Houston Oilers

20-17

NFL NUMBER ONE DRAFT CHOICE

Ernie Davis
halfback

Syracuse to
Washington
Redskins

BASKET

Wilt Cham

FIRST PLAYER TO SCORE 100 POINTS IN A SINGLE GAME

Philadelphia Warrior **Wilt** the St

SCORING LEADER
SEASON

50.4 average
4,029 points

SCORING LEADER
SINGLE GAME

100 points
Philadelphia versus the **New York Knicks**
Game is played in Hershey, Pennsylvania.
The fans go wild, forcing the referees to call
the game with 46 seconds left on the clock.

WHAT A YEAR IT WAS!

BALL
berlain

FIRST PLAYER TO SCORE OVER
4,000 POINTS
IN A SEASON

A slam dunk!

eaks one NBA record after another

FIELD GOALS	REBOUNDS	
SINGLE GAME	SEASON	
36	25.7 average	

FREE THROWS
SINGLE GAME

28 out of 32

WHAT A YEAR IT WAS!

1962 BASKETBALL news

NBA CHAMPIONS
Boston Celtics
over
LA Lakers
4-3

NBA ROOKIE OF THE YEAR
Walt Bellamy
Chicago Packers

NBA MOST VALUABLE PLAYER
Bill Russell
Boston Celtics

NCAA CHAMPIONS
Cincinnati
over
Ohio State
71- 59

NBA ALL-STAR GAME
WEST over **EAST**
150-130

MVP
Bob Pettit, St. Louis

NCAA REBOUNDS
Jerry Lucas
Ohio State
21.1 average

The **Boston Celtics** capture their sixth straight Eastern Division title and a record fourth straight NBA title.

6 ft. 5-1/2 in. Princeton man **Bill Bradley** is considered the best Ivy League player in years.

John Wooden is head coach at UCLA.

San Francisco becomes the new home of the **Philadelphia Warriors**.

Bob Cousy of the Boston Celtics sets a NBA record as he makes his 5,926th field goal.

The American Basketball League is disbanded after only one year.

BOXING—1962

HEAVYWEIGHT
Floyd Patterson
Sonny Liston

MIDDLEWEIGHT
Terry Downes
Paul Pender

WELTERWEIGHT
Benny "Kid" Paret
Emile Griffith

FEATHERWEIGHT
Davey Moore

LIGHTWEIGHT
Joe Brown
Carlos Ortiz

LIGHT HEAVYWEIGHT
Archie Moore
Harold Johnson

NEWS

◆ Emile Griffith regains the welterweight title he lost last year to **Benny "Kid" Paret** after beating Paret into a state of insensibility. Paret never regains consciousness and dies ten days after the fight.

◆ In what is billed as the *"fight of the decade"* Sonny Liston KO's Floyd Patterson in two minutes and six seconds of the first round and walks off with the world heavyweight title.

chess

WORLD CHAMPION
Mikhail Botvinnik
U.S.S.R.

U.S. CHAMPION
Larry Evans

Bobby Fischer

BOWLING

BPAA ALL-STAR TOURNAMENT
Dick Weber
Shirley Garms

ABC MASTERS TOURNAMENT
Billy Golembiewski

BOWLER OF THE YEAR
Don Carter

WORLD'S INVITATIONAL
Don Carter
Marion Ladewig

BOWLING NEWS
The National Bowling League, formed last year, is dismantled.

WHAT A YEAR IT WAS!

167

1962 — *Jack Nicklaus*
Wins U.S. Open

This is the biggest professional victory of his career which was launched when he finished 50th in the Los Angeles Open winning $33.33.

A new golf star flashes across the horizon as Jack Nicklaus holes out to take the U.S. Open title.

A jubilant moment.

Golf

U.S. OPEN	PGA/LPGA LEADING MONEY WINNER
Jack Nicklaus	Arnold Palmer $81,448
Murle McKenzie Lindstrom	Mickey Wright $21,641

WHAT A YEAR IT WAS!

Arnold Palmer — 1962
Wins British Open

The usually staid British crowd stampedes for positions on the last green as Palmer prepares to sink his last putt.

It gives Palmer a closing 69 and a final score that breaks the record for the 102-year-old championship.

Nicklaus beats Arnold Palmer in the U.S. Open, but Palmer is the master here.

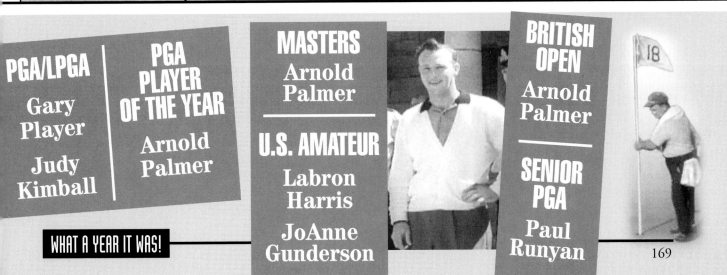

PGA/LPGA

Gary Player

Judy Kimball

PGA PLAYER OF THE YEAR

Arnold Palmer

MASTERS

Arnold Palmer

U.S. AMATEUR

Labron Harris

JoAnne Gunderson

BRITISH OPEN

Arnold Palmer

SENIOR PGA

Paul Runyan

WHAT A YEAR IT WAS!

169

Kentucky
Governor
Bert Combs and
100,000 fans witness a thrilling Kentucky Derby.

Coming in for
the home stretch.

Suddenly
Number 3,
Decidedly,
shoots up on
the outside to
take the "Run for the Roses" with a new Derby record.

Four horses, including ***Admiral's Voyage*** and ***Ridan*** are battling down the stretch.

Two weeks later there is a dual to the wire in the Preakness at Baltimore as ***Greek Money*** moves up on the rail to battle ***Ridan*** to the wire.

R**idan*'s jockey claims ***Greek Money fouled him but the claim is disallowed and ***Greek Money*** winds up with top money.

170

WHAT A YEAR IT WAS!

racing

The third leg of the Triple Crown,
New York's Belmont, is another thriller.

With *Admiral's Voyage* on the rail and *Jaipur*
on the outside, *Jaipur* gets past the rail first
by a whisker.

KENTUCKY DERBY

Decidedly
ridden by **Bill Hartack**

PREAKNESS

Greek Money
ridden by **John Rotz**

BELMONT STAKES

Jaipur
ridden by
Willie Shoemaker

HORSE OF THE YEAR

Kelso

MONEY LEADERS

Jockey
Bill Shoemaker
$2,916,844

Horse
Never Bend
$402,969

Racing News

A jockey for 31 of his
46 years and winner of 4,779
races, **Eddie Arcaro** retires as
the greatest money-winning
rider in the history of horse
racing, bringing in $30 million
of which he received 10%.

Famous Births

- Bo Jackson
- Darryl Strawberry
- Evander Holyfield
- Herschel Walker
- Jackie Joyner-Kersee
- Patrick Ewing
- Roger Clemens
- Tracy Austin
- William "Refrigerator" Perry

TENNIS

U.S. OPEN

Rod Laver over **Roy Emerson**

Margaret Smith over **Darlene Hard**

WIMBLEDON

Rod Laver over **Marty Mulligan**

Karen Hantze Susman over **Vera Sukova**

DAVIS CUP

Australia over **Mexico**, 5-0

TENNIS NEWS

Australia's **Rod Laver** becomes the second man in history to win the grand slam of amateur tennis — U.S., French, Australian and Wimbledon titles — equaling the 1938 feat of American Don Budge.

SWIMMING

DAWN FRASER becomes first women to swim 100 meters in under 1:00.

FRED BALDASARE is the first to swim the English Channel underwater.

HOCKEY

STANLEY CUP CHAMPIONS

TORONTO MAPLE LEAFS over CHICAGO BLACKHAWKS, 4-2

ROSS TROPHY
(Leading Scorer)

BOBBY HULL, Chicago

VEZINA TROPHY
(Outstanding Goalie)

JACQUES PLANTE, Montreal

CALDER MEMORIAL TROPHY
(Rookie Of The Year)

BOBBY ROUSSEAU, Montreal

LADY BYNG MEMORIAL TROPHY
(Most Gentlemanly Player)

DAVE KEON, Toronto

HART MEMORIAL TROPHY
(MVP)

JACQUES PLANTE, Montreal

WORLD CHAMPIONS

Sweden

WHAT A YEAR IT WAS!

CAR RACING

INDIANAPOLIS 500
RODGER WARD
Leader Card 500 Roadster, 140.293 mph

LE MANS
OLIVER GENDEBIEN & PHIL HILL
Ferrari 250, 115.22 mph

WINSTON CUP
JOE WEATHERLY

TRACK & FIELD

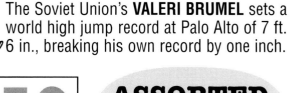

BOSTON MARATHON
Eino Oksanen, Finland (third win)

HIGH JUMP
The Soviet Union's **VALERI BRUMEL** sets a world high jump record at Palo Alto of 7 ft. 6 in., breaking his own record by one inch.

cycling
TOUR de FRANCE
Jacques Anquetil
France (third win)

RODEO

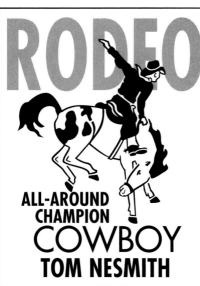

ALL-AROUND CHAMPION COWBOY TOM NESMITH

ASSORTED AWARDS

AP ATHLETE OF THE YEAR
Maury Wills (Baseball)
Dawn Fraser (Swimming)

THE HICKOCK BELT
Maury Wills
(Baseball)

Figure Skating

WORLD CHAMPIONS
Donald Jackson
Canada

Sjoukje Dijkstra
Holland

U.S. CHAMPIONS
Monty Hoyt

Barbara Roles Pursley

SOCCER
Brazil over **Czechoslovakia**
3-1

SOCCER NEWS
Brazil's soccer star **Pele** is declared a national treasure.

DOG SHOW WINNER
WESTMINSTER KENNEL CLUB
Best-In-Show
Elfinbrook Simon

West Highland White Terrier

1962 WAS A GREAT YEAR, BUT...

THE BEST IS YET TO COME!